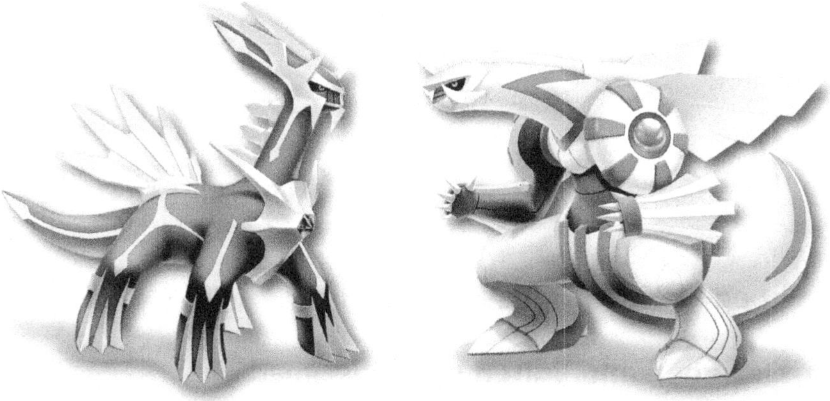

NINTENDO SWITCH GAMING GUIDE II

DETAILS

First Published in 2023 by Old Mate Media.

Written, Designed and Edited by: Chris Stead
Produced by: Kate Stead
Published by: Old Mate Media

Paperback ISBN: 978-1-922740-13-7
Paperback (B&W Edition) ISBN: 978-1-922740-16-8
Hardback ISBN: 978-1-922740-14-4
Digital ISBN: 978-1-922740-15-1

FIRST EDITION

INTRODUCTION

Welcome to Volume 2 of my Nintendo Switch Gaming Guide series. My name is Chris Stead, and I've been one of the world's leading games journalists since the mid-nineties. In fact, my first published reviews began appearing in N64 Gamer, one of Australia's most beloved magazines. It's hard to believe it was focused on the great, great, great grandfather of the Nintendo Switch console.

That makes me feel old!

I've covered every single Nintendo launch since then, getting behind-closed-doors early access to the hardware, the software and the developers along the way.

During that time, I've run the Australian arm of Game Informer, the world's biggest games magazine. I was also editor of Australian GamePro, Editor-in-Chief of Gameplayer and have been involved with the launch and content for countless other publications and websites. IGN, Gamespot, Kotaku, Rooster Teeth, Fandom and many more.

But perhaps, more importantly, I'm a gamer and a father of gamers. Those memories I have playing Super Mario Bros. in the early eighties are now being enjoyed by my kids, although with the far more expansive Super Mario Odyssey.

I look at Nintendo and gaming in general now with the same passion, but see it through a different lens. I want my children to love gaming, too, but it's more challenging now than it was when I was a kid. Now you're online with thousands of strangers, there's microtransactions in games, violence can look very realistic, and developers have refined their systems to encourage addiction.

To help, I've created this guide. It's designed to give both parents and their kids an insight into some of the best experiences they can have with Nintendo, and to do so with eyes wide open to what these experiences offer. I hope this allows people to save money by making smart game purchases that work within their boundaries and for their tastes.

If you haven't already, it's wise to start with Volume I. In that book I cover a lot of the basics about the Nintendo Switch and its official peripherals. As well as detail the best, kid-friendly games from the first third of the Nintendo Switch's lifetime. There's also a handful of cheats to help get you on your way.

In Volume II of the Nintendo Switch Gaming Guide, I focused on everything that has happed through the COVID era. So that's mid-2020 into 2022. I run through the latest batch of great games and accessories for the Nintendo Switch, as well as explore some of the key news and big questions that have emerged in gaming.

And don't worry, Volume III isn't far away, which will bring you up to the latest and greatest releases. **Make sure you follow my Amazon author profile** to get first access.

I hope you enjoy the read.

Chris Stead

TRANSPARENCY

In this book I provide honest commentary on a host of games and accessories based on my own personal experiences and research. In most cases, these products were sent to me by their makers for the purpose of review. This is standard practice within games journalism.

Where applicable you'll see a link to where these items can be purchased on Amazon. In my travels, I've found Amazon to be on most occasions the cheapest place to buy these products. It's available in almost all countries. And it's also likely where you purchased this guide in the first place.

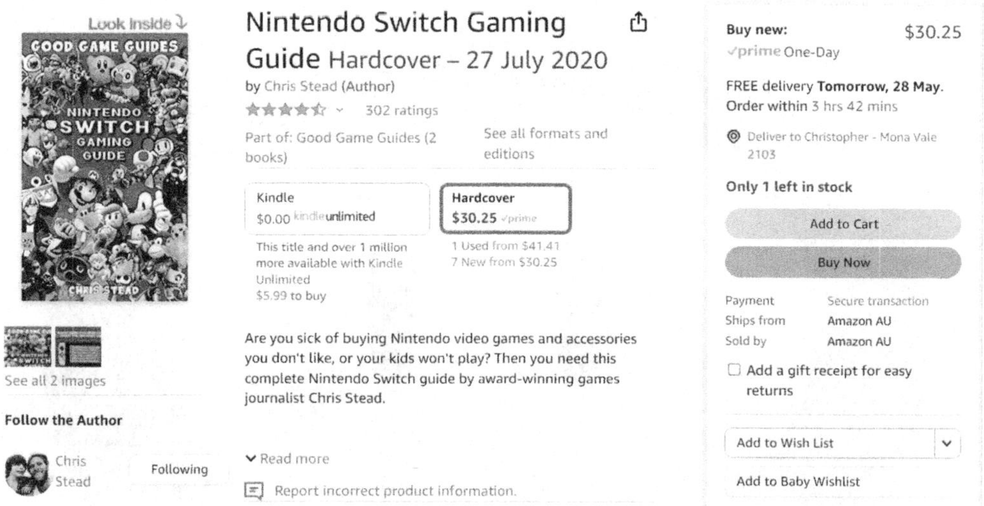

The links are there for your convenience, and if you follow them, I might be eligible to receive a minor kickback from Amazon for sending them the business. This is a small way I can help offset the cost of creating this guide. However, its existence in no way influences the content chosen for this guide or the way it is written.

This guide is about offering you a wide and deep comparison of options. This includes many indie games you cannot buy on Amazon.

Also, **please remember** that this guide is written for kids and their parents. While there's plenty of insights here that I hope can help gamers of all ages, please be mindful that the content choice, style, tone and detail reflects my target audiences. Hence the lack of adult-focused games and kid-speak words like "cool."

Thank you for your understanding and support.

VOLUME 1

There is no overlap in information between my first Nintendo Switch book, and Volume 2. If you're just starting out with the console or are looking for the best games from early in its lifespan, you may want to start there. It's available on Amazon and is a free read for Kindle Unlimited members.

Just scan the QR code.

What is the Nintendo Switch OLED?

The Nintendo Switch hardware has been updated. It had long been rumoured, but when it finally arrived, it wasn't quite the upgrade many gamers had been hoping for. On October 8, 2021, the Nintendo Switch (OLED) become available globally.

Here in Australia, the price is AU$539.95, and in the USA it's US$350. Obviously, it will be different depending on your location, but one constant is that it costs around 15% more than the standard Switch model. At least at launch.

It's important to note this is not the Nintendo Switch Pro that had been anticipated. It doesn't feature a leap in internal power to help it better compete with the visual, audio and performance prowess of the PlayStation 5 or Xbox Series X consoles. It's ever so slightly longer (9.4 to 9.5-inches) and a tiny bit heavier (390g to 420g), but more-or-less takes up the same footprint.

What you do get is a bigger and more vibrant screen thanks to its OLED panel. Yes, the Switch OLED is the same size as the original model, but there is less of a border around the screen. As such there's now 7-inches of screen real estate, up from the 6.62-inches of the original Switch. The resolution remains the same, however, at 1280 × 720 pixels.

The other notable improvement is an increase in the internal storage, doubling from 32GB to 64GB. Outside of that, you can enjoy improved speakers, and a better stand at the back that provides more angles to position the Switch. The Nintendo Switch (OLED) comes in a Neon or a Black & White colour scheme, too.

The shorthand of all this information is that newcomers buying into the Switch ecosystem for the first time might as well get the OLED model. It plays the same games, but they do look much better on the Switch screen. And the extra storage is certainly a bonus.

However, if you already own a Nintendo Switch, it's not worth upgrading unless you exclusively play in handheld mode. The experience playing a Switch on a TV is effectively unchanged. And with no leap in raw power and the same battery life, unless you're playing in handheld mode the majority of the time, you simply won't get the return in investment.

Nintendo Switch Lite vs Switch OLED

The new Nintendo Switch (OLED) isn't the first time Nintendo has added to its available console models. Previously, there was the Nintendo Switch Lite. As its name suggests, it's a fair bit smaller than the other two models. The screen, while the same resolution, is only 5.5-inches and the device weighs only 270g.

It's designed to be purely a mobile device and is targeted at gamers who want to play the Switch in handheld mode only. The Joy-Cons are even built-in to the device and cannot be detached — a risky proposition given that they do wear out quicker than I'd like and tend to get stick drift after a while. Plus, the reduced size does result in a smaller battery life, which is a little counter intuitive.

The good news is that as a result of the trimmings, the Nintendo Switch Lite is a fair bit cheaper than the original Switch model and the new OLED model. About 25% to 30% cheaper, depending on the sales when you're looking to buy. And it does play all the same games at the same quality.

So, if you never intend to use your Nintendo Switch on a TV, but rather just on the go in handheld mode, it's certainly worth considering. But if you can pony up for the OLED model, you will get a much better experience thanks to the battery life and fantastic screen.

For more, check out my comparison video on all the Switch models. It's designed to help parents and you can find it on YouTube, just make your way to **www.youtube.com/@daydrinkingdad/**.

New Handheld Console... Kind Of

In a bit of a surprise, Nintendo released a new version of its old-school Game & Watch handheld on November 12, 2021. That would be the Game & Watch from the early eighties!

It allows you to play the first two Zelda games — The Legend of Zelda and Zelda II: The Adventure of Link — as well as the Game Boy version of The Legend of Zelda: Link's Awakening. In addition, there is a little arcade game that makes the clock playable and an interactive timer themed to Zelda II. The original Game & Watch title that starred Zelda's hero Link, Vermin, is also included.

It's all very nostalgic, but it's also kind of cool. Something of a collectable. It's not too expensive either. Around the same price as a game, depending on where you are in the world.

Special Edition Switch Consoles

If you are considering buying into the Nintendo Switch family, there's now quite a collection of special edition consoles out there you can consider. And there will be plenty more over the coming years as well. Special Edition consoles don't have any differences in terms of performance, but offer aesthetic variances usually themed to certain games.

On most occasions this involves some art on the base station and/or some unique colouring to the Joy-Con controllers. They can often be a bit lazy in my opinion, but if you have a huge love for a specific game series, it can bring some extra flair to your living room and an added sense of pride.

The main problem you will face with Special Edition Switch consoles is that they're not as easy to come by as the standard fare. Some of them were only ever released for a limited time, so loiter unpredictably in retail outlets or need to be hunted down through online stores. Potentially even second-hand.

As of mid-2023, there have been 23 Special Edition Switch consoles. Here is a list of what you can get.

- Animal Crossing: New Horizons Switch
- Diablo 3 Eternal Collection Nintendo Switch
- Dialga & Palkia Lite
- Disney Tsum Tsum Festival Bundle
- Dragon Quest XI Nintendo Switch
- Fortnite Special Edition Switch
- Jack Jeanne Switch Lite
- Legend of Zelda: Tears of the Kingdom OLED
- Mario Red + Blue Edition Nintendo Switch
- Mickey and Friends Disney Tsum Tsum
- Monster Hunter Rise Edition
- Monster Hunter XX Special Edition Nintendo Switch Bundle
- Nintendo Labo Switch
- Pokémon Let's Go Pikachu / Eevee Nintendo Switch
- Pokémon Lite
- Pokémon Scarlet & Violet OLED
- Pokémon Sword and Shield Switch Lite
- Splatoon 2 Nintendo Switch
- Splatoon 3 OLED
- Super Mario Odyssey Nintendo Switch
- Super Smash Bros. Ultimate Nintendo Switch
- Trials of Mana (very rare)
- Zacian and Zamazenta Nintendo Switch Lite

Alternative Switch Controllers

What I love most about the Nintendo Switch is that it puts couch multiplayer at the forefront of the experience. While Microsoft and Sony have both pushed further and further away from offline multiplayer experiences over recent console generations, the Nintendo Switch embraces these experiences.

Playing games with friends and siblings, in the same room, were some of the most enjoyable times of my formative years. I want my kids to enjoy the same thrills.

However, that does require extra controllers. You can, of course, go official. The Nintendo Switch Pro controller is very solid and dependable. Plus, it gives you all the bells and whistles, such as Amiibo support, IR, rumble and motion controls. But it's expensive!

The Joy-Con is less awesome. They tend to get drift in the analogue sticks, which means that it will always be tilting one way or the other just a bit, even when not in use. And smaller kids can peel off the rubber nubs too easily. At least the Joy-Con can easily be replaced, except on the Nintendo Switch Lite console.

Both the official options are leagues ahead of the cheap third-party offerings you can pick up off places like eBay and Amazon. I've made the error of buying those myself; wasted money! They're flimsy, easily break and have terrible battery life.

There are, however, some quality, third-party Nintendo Switch controllers that are worth considering. Controllers from known, respected brands. These not only offer great build quality and battery life, but features beyond what you can get with the official controllers. Here are a few I've come across that are worth considering.

8BitDo SN30 Pro 2

Despite its retro look, this alternative controller to the Nintendo Switch Pro is full of modern, pro-gamer goodness. It feels great in your hand, with a nice textured back, awesome sticks and triggers, and a balanced, solid weight. There are two additional flipper buttons on the back as well as a toggle to swap between button layout profiles. However, there's no traditional shoulder buttons.

You manage the profiles through an awesome mobile app that allows you to customise everything. You can alter the button mapping, stick sensitivity, vibrations, trigger depth and more. The battery lasts 20-hours and the SN30 Pro 2 even has motion-sensors built in. As it connects via Bluetooth, you can also use it on a PC, Mac, tablet or mobile phone as well.

PDP Faceoff Deluxe+ Audio Wired Controller

If you don't mind a wired controller — which is highly dependent on how close your Switch is situated to your couch — then you may want to consider the PDP Faceoff Deluxe+. It's reasonably priced, while still offering the robust build, and sturdy sticks and buttons you need for genuine longevity. It even has smartly placed, extra programmable buttons to give you added in-game input options.

It's big selling point, however, is that it comes with a built-in audio jack. This means you can plug in a pair of headphones for better sounding games and even voice chat, where it is supported by a game. So, if you love online shooters like Fortnite (for voice chat) or need a good audio solution for your Switch, this controller can tick two boxes at once.

It's just a shame you can't remove the wire should you want to use it in standard wireless form, and it's important to note this controller doesn't have rumble support.

PowerA Enhanced Wireless Controller

Personally, I'm a fan of rechargeable controllers as it's a lot better for the environment, but boy can it become a hassle with the kids. They never remember to plug the things in, then suddenly there's four kids who want to play and four dead controllers that need to be charged (in four different ports).

The PowerA controllers revert to the traditional AA-battery approach, circumnavigating this problem. Even if they create another for old Mother Earth.

In your hands, it feels the most like the Switch Pro controller of all the alternatives. It loses the rumble, IR and Amiibo NFC features, but it retains motion controls. It also offers two extra programmable buttons and a range of themed versions (mostly based around Pokémon.) It's a fair bit cheaper than the official controller, too.

It's worth noting that you will also find a Nano version of this controller. It's effectively the same device, but in a smaller form factor. For the youngest humans whose hands are still growing, the Nano is a good option as its easier for them to get their fingers in the right spot.

Beboncool Switch Pro Controller

If you're big on your Amiibo collection and the features they unlock, then you may want to look at the Beboncool Switch Pro Controller.

Not only does it have the NFC feature, but it has rumble support and motion controls. You'll also find a customisable Turbo button, which can give you a bit of extra flex in challenging games, and a dedicated screen capture button.

The button and stick feel isn't quite as good as the other options on this list, which is likely why it is a fair bit cheaper than the official Pro Controller. The d-pad, in particular, is more button-based than pad, which isn't to everyone's liking.

Be aware that there is a version of the Beboncool controller that comes in light blue or orange colouring, but is best identified by its PlayStation inspired layout. So that's the two sticks at the bottom. This doesn't come with the NFC feature, however. So, if Amiibo is your thing, it's best to stick with the red and blue option, which has the Xbox inspired layout.

Note: Since I first wrote this stroy, I've noticed stock can be hard to find. It's hard to know if this is a temporary issue or not.

What are the Best Games on Switch Vol 2?

Below you will find a curated list of great games that are available on the Nintendo Switch, and what experience they will offer to you and your kids. They are in alphabetical order, and are largely made up of titles that came out after mid-2020 and through COVID.

For a guide to the best games that came out prior to that date, I recommend picking up the first volume in this series. And for games post-COVID, look to Volume 3.

Nintendo passed the 120 million Switch units sold mark in 2023, which is quite the achievement. As part of that announcement, the company also revealed it's top-selling games of all time on the console. How many do you have?

1. **Mario Kart 8 Deluxe** (53.79 million units)
2. **Animal Crossing: New Horizons** (42.21 million units)
3. **Super Smash Bros. Ultimate** (31.09 million units)
4. **The Legend of Zelda: Breath of the Wild** (29.81 million units)
5. **Pokémon Sword and Shield** (25.82 million units)
6. **Super Mario Odyssey** (25.76 million units)
7. **Pokémon Scarlet and Violet** (22.10 million units)
8. **Super Mario Party** (19.14 million units)
9. **New Super Mario Bros. U Deluxe** (15.41 million units)
10. **Ring Fit Adventure** (15.38 million units)

I've also made an effort to provide you with some insights into the

type of player best suited to each game. Look for the key, similar to the one below, which provides some view to what you can expect from a game's experience.

Age Range = All, Middle or Older. (Older being around ten and over).
Local Multiplayer = Yes (Good for families with multiple kids).
Difficulty = Easy, Medium or Hard (with respect to kids' skill levels).
Genre = A broad summation of the kind of gameplay experience.

You can click the Buy It Now link to jump out and purchase a game that fits your need. Some games are only available as downloadable products through the Nintendo eShop. You access this on the console itself, so there is no link I can provide for those titles. You do not need to have a Nintendo Switch Online subscription in order to buy games from the eShop.

Alex Kidd in Miracle World DX

Age Range = All
Local Multiplayer = No
Difficulty = Medium
Genre = Platformer

Every kid who grew up in the 90s played Alex Kidd in Miracle World. It came for free with the Sega Master System II, which was a super popular console at the time. It looked like a classic sidescrolling platformer, except you'd often get vehicles to control, you do all your fighting with one giant fist, and some fights are decided by paper, scissors, rock.

It was also tough, as you only got a handful of lives to get through all 17 stages and, once they were gone, you had to start again. Proper old school! At least as you progressed you could pick up money that you'd spend at a shop for bonus gear, helping you on your way.

It's really exciting to see this great game come back. You can opt to play with the original retro graphics or new modern visuals. The modern graphics look sharp if cartoony. Plus, the developer has added some new levels and alternate boss fights so there is even more content to enjoy.

We even love the new music and sound effects. A great remake, but beware, it's still tough. Not helped by the fact the controls aren't perfect!

Apex Legends

Age Range = Older | **Local Multiplayer** = No
Difficulty = Hard | **Genre** = Battle Royale

Apex Legends is a free-to-play Battle Royale game — like Fortnite — set in the same universe as the Titanfall series. There are no big Titan robot suits, however. Instead, you're a mercenary fighting it out on a great big island — your multiplayer battlefield. Well initially, anyway. In the nearly 20 seasons since launch, we've got additional battlefields to play in, as well as an Arena mode that allows for more traditional 3v3 battles, and plenty more.

But it's made its name with its Battle Royale gameplay. Apex Legends offers plenty of neat ideas that separate it from Fortnite. There are 20 squads of three players on the map, which means 60 total. There were six customisable characters to choose from at launch, each with their own special abilities. That's very different to Fortnite, where everyone is the same except for their appearance. As of the time of writing there are now 18 characters and rising.

There different abilities play a pivotal role in our combat unfolds. Some can turn invisible, some can mark enemies, others can heal,

there's one who can create ziplines, another which can track enemy locations, and so forth. This creates an interesting RPG-like experience, where you need to assemble your team smartly and think about how to apply your abilities together on the battlefield.

Much more will be added to this game over time, but if you like the idea of Fortnite with a more realistic aesthetic, it's worth a look now.

BALAN WONDERLAND

Age Range = All | **Local Multiplayer** = Yes
Difficulty = Medium | **Genre** = Adventure

As soon as this game was announced I was excited about it. After all, it's made by RPG legends Square Enix, but it's a 3D platformer. So, you get the wonders of a magical RPG with the action of a Mario game. Cool, right?

There's certainly plenty of imagination in this game, with 12 incredibly varied themed worlds that make you feel like you're playing in a dream. The cartoony, colourful graphics help create a great atmosphere, as does Balan, the strange individual who summons heroes Leo and Emma into his Wonderworld.

As two heroes would suggest, you can enjoy this game in co-op, and while a lot of the game is classic platforming, there's a fun fashion twist that makes the game feel quite unique. You need to find and put on costumes, which give you the abilities you need to solve puzzles, beat bosses and explore. And there's a whopping 80 costumes to try!

Just the type of adventure kids — and the young at heart — can enjoy.

Big Rumble Boxing: Creed Champions

Age Range = Middle | **Local Multiplayer** = Yes
Difficulty = Medium **Genre** = Fighting

A fighting game set in the Rocky universe must be fun, right? Big Rumble Boxing features 20 characters to choose from across the Rocky and Creed movies, including famous names like Rocky Balboa, Apollo Creed and Ivan Drago.

There's a story to play through with each fighter, which is a nice touch, but it's a shame that it's only told through text. It's neat, however, that you can do some of the famous training sessions from the films. They're actually a lot of fun, despite effectively being minigames.

The gameplay takes an arcade approach, which makes it easier to pick up and play. Each character has different speeds and movements, so you'll need to mix up your strategy and think of new ways to fight each opponent. If you build up your special meter, you can unleash a unique special attack, too.

But the key to winning is all about counters, combos and timing blocks. There's not a lot of modes, but you can play against a friend, which is the best experience anyway.

Cadence of Hyrule - Crypt of the NecroDancer

Age Range = Older | **Local Multiplayer** = Yes
Difficulty = Hard | **Genre** = Roguelite

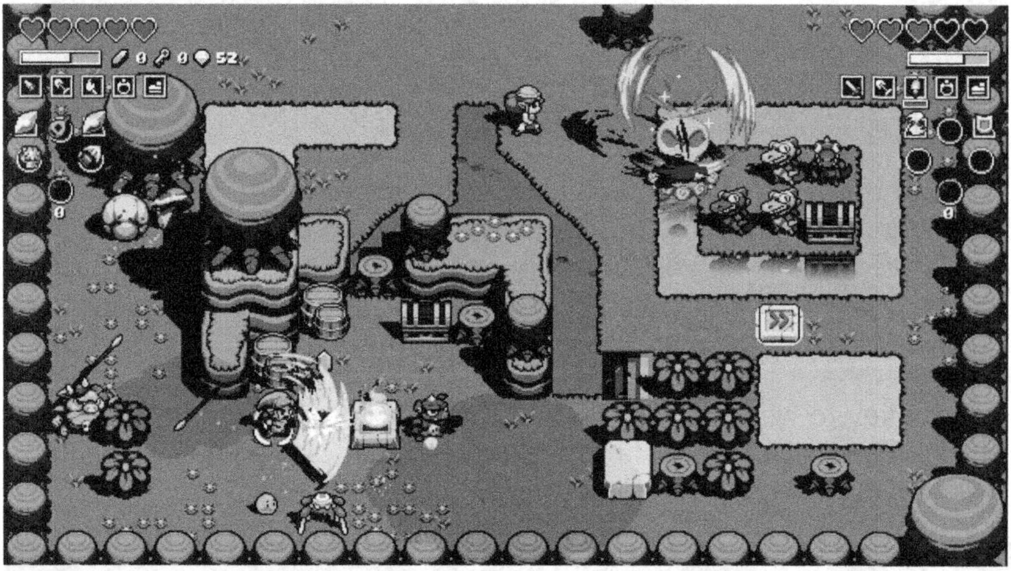

If you're a huge Zelda fan looking for a way to fill in the time until Breath of the Wild 2, then you could try out Cadence of Hyrule. Although it's a very different kind of game. It takes the gameplay of indie favourite Crypt of the NecroDancer — a mix of roguelite dungeon crawling and music rhythm — and combines it with Zelda's world of Hyrule. All while looking like the original top-down games from Zelda's SNES era.

It's a team-up I never would have expected to work, but it manages to give both series a breath of fresh air.

You play as Cadence, who has been magically transported from Crypt of the NecroDancer to Hyrule and must help Link and Zelda defeat a music-loving bad guy.

The maps look very inspired by Zelda A Link to the Past, but are actually randomly generated each time you play, with elements moving in unpredictable ways.

What makes this game so unique though is that you need to move and attack in time with the music. And said music is an awesome remix of old Zelda tunes. A rhythm roguelike then!

Enemy types have different attacks, but those within the same type have the same attack. So individually they are predictable... they just never attack solo. As such, combat with multiple foes becomes this weird dance as you move in time with the beat to solve the battle rhythm.

It's easier than it sounds, but remains very rewarding. Especially as major items and weapons stay with you as you progress — unusual for roguelites — and only lesser objects are lost on death. So, it's just forgiving enough to be enjoyed by all ages.

Crash Bandicoot 4: It's About Time

Age Range = All | **Local Multiplayer** = Yes
Difficulty = Easy | **Genre** = Platformer

For the past 22 years — which is how long it has been since Crash Bandicoot 3 — bad dudes Dr. Neo Cortex and Doctor N. Tropy have been imprisoned on an asteroid. However, they use a rip in time to escape and yet again start causing havoc.

Crash and his sister Coco spin into action with the help of five quantum masks. As you unlock these, you also access their unique powers. One gives you invincibility, another helps you switch objects in and out of reality, a third can freeze time and then there is one that flips gravity.

Finally, there is one that puts you into a spin so fast you can zip across stages, jump high and break objects.

There's a host of collectables in each stage, too, and a range of exciting modes. The latter includes multiplayer, time trials, levels where you get to play as the baddies and an N.Verted mode that has you replay every stage with reverse controls and graphics.

We also must mention the cool levels, which not only look great, but head to different eras in time giving you plenty of exciting places to explore. Excellent.

Cruis'n Blast

Age Range = All | **Local Multiplayer** = Yes
Difficulty = Easy | **Genre** = Racing

We love a good arcade racer and the Cruis'n series has been killing it for decades. Usually, you'll find it in arcades, but this time you get to play it at home.

Like all racing games, the goal here is to come first in the point to point races. What makes Cruis'n Blast stand out is that the 24 themed tracks are just ridiculously over the top and fun. You'll be driving through deserts getting blown apart by tornados one second, then smashing through the ice in the snowy mountains while a giant Yeti tries to grab you the next.

All while doing huge jumps, barrel rolls, flips, drifts, boosts, wheelies and other stunts while battling aggressive AI opponents.

Even the 20 unlockable vehicles get bizarre: you'll race as a unicorn, a dinosaur or even a UFO. Some of the tracks are a bit short and reuse sections, so it can get a little repetitive once you have finished the main tour. However, you can play four-player local multiplayer!

DESCENDERS

Age Range = Middle | **Local Multiplayer** = No
Difficulty = Medium | **Genre** = Sports

Descenders has you descending (get it?) on a mountain bike down some crazy randomly generated hills. You never know what's going to be over the next jump, round a muddy bend or behind a big tree. Yep, this is an extreme cycling video game with the focus on extreme.

You can play Descenders in third-person or first-person for a very cool challenge. You can play online with up to eight-people, too, if you like. As you go through the world map choosing different run types to try your only real goal is to get to the bottom, but you can improve your reputation (which lets you unlock more stuff) by busting tricks.

You have to be careful not to crash too many times, too, as you do have health that will run out. This gives the game a cool survival element, as you can't just go fast; you have to expertly balance your speed and your landings or you'll get smashed.

The visuals are pretty good for an indie game, too, ensuring this is one game not to miss.

DESTROY ALL HUMANS!

Age Range = Older | **Local Multiplayer** = No
Difficulty = Medium | **Genre** = Action Adventure

It's not too often you get to play the bad guy, but it's always fun. In Destroy All Humans! you get to play a classic bad guy stereotype in an invading alien, and the developer has a tonne of fun with the concept.

You play a truly evil alien clone who has arrived in 1950's USA with the goal of taking DNA from humans. Of course, his presence quickly gets the military and government involved, who are trying to track you down as you roam across neighbourhoods causing carnage.

There's a truly awesome sense of humour to this game, with a very silly story and over-the-top characters. The amazing array of weapons and the general gameplay — like using telepathy to hurl cows at policeman — will have you giggling for hours.

There's plenty of variety, too, with the ability to fly UFOs and jetpacks, and use bizarre alien powers. Meanwhile, the large open world is filled with lots of fun pop references and looks great despite this being a remake. Yes, being bad can be fun.

Dice Legacy

Age Range = Middle | **Local Multiplayer** = No
Difficulty = Medium | **Genre** = Strategy

Here's a unique game experience for those of you willing to try something different. Dice Legacy offers a strange mix of genres. It's part city builder, part real-time strategy and even a bit like a classic tabletop game.

Your ship arrives on an uncharted ringworld — it's literally a ring! — and you're tasked with staking a claim, building a settlement and not getting overwhelmed by the obstacles and challenges that come at you. Building your township is where the fun starts and it all comes down to rolling dice. Depending on what you roll you can gather resources, construct, explore, defend and more.

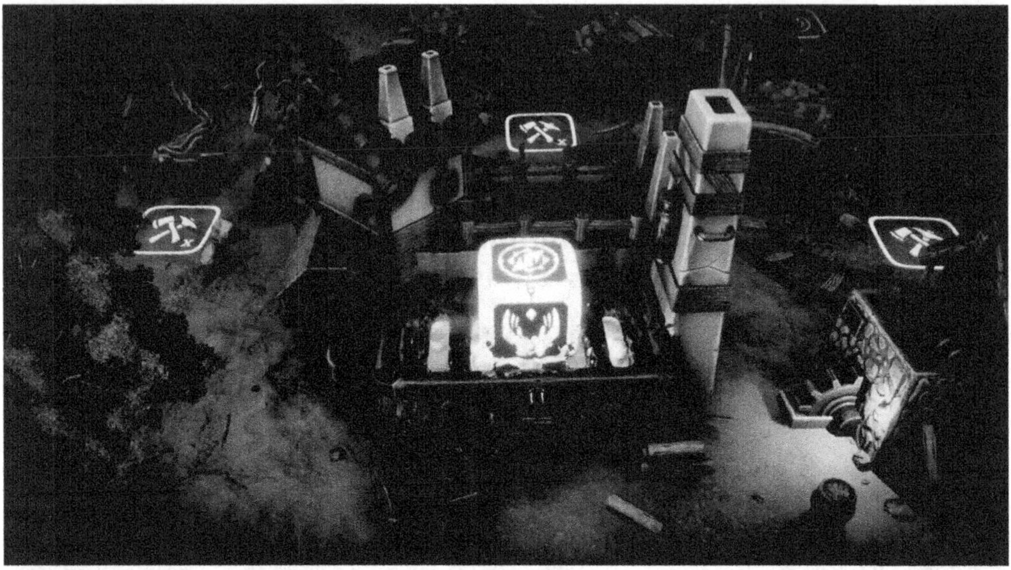

As you go this mechanic just gets deeper and deeper because you begin to specialise your units and buildings. As you beat a challenge, harder ones unlock and this can get quite immersive, too. Especially as seasonal conditions impact the way unit and building abilities work.

You also unlock new heroes, which give you different dice to roll adding yet another layer to the strategy. It's a good-looking game, too! Definitely worth a play!

Dragon Ball Z: Kakarot

Age Range = Older | **Local Multiplayer** = No
Difficulty = Medium | **Genre** = Action-RPG

Any new Dragon Ball game is grounds for excitement, but the latest entry is not just another fighter. This is a proper, action-RPG. There is a big world to explore, with an over-map that you can use to quickly fly between larger locations — which includes towns — which each deliver plenty to discover and characters to meet.

There's sidequests, levelling-up, items to equip and even various abilities to shift between. So very much an RPG in that sense.

There's a story, too, of course. Fans of the anime will love it, as every chapter plays out like an episode from the show. But this is a Dragon Ball game, so there is still plenty of fighting. In fact, combat plays out very similar to the 3D fighting games in the series, with big arenas, spectacular effects and all the strategy we love.

So, this game basically has all the fighting fun, as well as a big RPG experience to dive into between the battles. Not to mention you can cook, hunt, fish, drive, fly, mine, trade and more.

After launch, developer Namco Bandai added a free multiplayer mode to the game, too. It's called Dragon Ball Card Warriors, and it's inspired by the awesome game Hearthstone. In it you collect a deck of Dragon Ball cards and then play them in traditional CCG style battles on series-themed boards.

Its existence is welcomed as it gets you better value and depth from your spend. However, be warned that while not required, this mode does feature microtransactions. It can only be played online, too, which is a bit of a shame.

DRAGON QUEST BUILDERS 2

Age Range = All | **Local Multiplayer** = No
Difficulty = Medium | **Genre** = Sandbox

Such is the success and love for Minecraft, that poor old sandbox game Dragon Quest Builders has often been overlooked. I say poor because it's an excellent building game that's superior to Minecraft in many ways.

As its name suggests, this game gets its world, items, enemies and characters from Square Enix's beloved Dragon Quest RPG series. But outside of that it's very much a creation game. Where it differs from Minecraft is that it provides a structure within which to play. You're not just on a randomly generated map trying to survive and build whatever you can imagine.

The map isn't randomly generated and there's a story to follow, one in which you must visit various islands, build whatever the people need, and then recruit followers to come back to your main island. This brings an RPG style progression system with it, where you constantly improve your character's crafting and building abilities.

While you can build whatever you want with the resources you harvest, there are blueprints to follow and quests to complete as you go. This sense of purpose, without squashing the pillars of creativity and crafting, works a treat. The deep controls and building options, and the need to protect your home base from enemies with fun hack 'n' slash gaming in between missions, keeps you glued to your screen for hours.

It doesn't hurt, of course, that the visuals are beautiful, colourful and sharp — a world away from Minecraft's pixel approach. There's also a companion character that comes with you on your adventure, helping with any tasks or fights you get into. It's a shame a friend can't be that companion in local co-op, but four people can team up together online.

DUNGEON DEFENDERS: AWAKENED

Age Range = Middle | **Local Multiplayer** = Yes
Difficulty = Medium | **Genre** = Action Strategy

The original Dungeon Defenders managed to forge a name for itself by making the most of combing two disparate genres. Third-person action combat and tower defence strategy gameplay. This unusual mix was kept simple, so it was easy to master, but then the complexity ramped up quickly, hooking you in and keeping you addicted.

With Dungeon Defenders: Awakened, the core gameplay concept is retained, just with more options available to you, making for a much richer gaming experience.

The tower defence part of the game goes first. You need to set up the traps and towers you think will best protect the Eternia Crystal from the enemies that are about to turn up in waves. When combat starts, you then attack directly with your character wherever your defences fail to do the job.

In between each round, you grab gems to upgrade your character, defences and equipment, and then you go again. Add awesome co-op play and vibrant visuals, and there's plenty of good reasons to give Dungeon Defenders a go.

Falconeer, The

Age Range = All | **Local Multiplayer** = No
Difficulty = Medium | **Genre** = Aerial Combat

We don't get too many aerial combat games nowadays, but one of the highlights in this genre is The Falconeer. It was originally a launch title for the Xbox Series X, but has since shifted onto other consoles.

The game has you riding on the back of a large warbird, wielding magic attacks in the fantasy world of The Great Ursee. This land has been devastated by climate change, leaving pockets of civilised and not so civilised islands amongst huge oceans.

It's a beautiful, relaxing place to explore. But mostly in which to fight.

The game controls much as you would expect from a flight game. You can swoop down to gain speed, bank left and right, do rolls and so forth. This genre is notoriously hard to play, but The Falconeer is refreshingly easy to pick-up.

The combat is awesome, too, plus side missions like escorts and fetch quests allow you to unlock better gear. It's the fantasy element,

however, that adds an enjoyable twist. You'll come across pirates and krakens and giant crabs. Eventually you can end up riding mounts like a dragon. And one of your key abilities is a lightning caster that needs to be charged by flying into thunderstorms.

There are multiple campaigns to go through, but strangely they're all tied to the same storyline. You basically get to play out the events from the perspectives of the four different factions that vie for control over Ursee. So just make sure you play them in order of worst warbird to best warbird, as the stats differ and it's annoying having to revert to a weaker bird midway through the game.

FUSER

Age Range = Middle | **Local Multiplayer** = No
Difficulty = Medium | **Genre** = Music

They're calling this the next evolution in the music game genre and it's hard to argue. After all, it's developed by the same guys who made the Rock Band series.

This time, the game puts you in charge of an entire music festival. You need to keep the crowd pumped and having fun from the opening act right through to the big name headliners. You can get very hands-on with the customisation, too. You can dress up your character, design the stage itself, decide on the pyrotechnics and choose the music.

There were over 100 tunes at launch and when you decide what will be in your set, you'll need to then place them on the decks with perfect timing to keep the crowd buzzing. You'll also need to control things like tempo. You can even mix in your own music in real-time.

It does take a little getting use to as the concept and controls are unique. But it's also stacks of fun just experimenting. There's even a co-op mode where you can mix music with three friends.

GAME BUILDER GARAGE

Age Range = Middle | **Local Multiplayer** = Yes
Difficulty = Medium | **Genre** = Sandbox

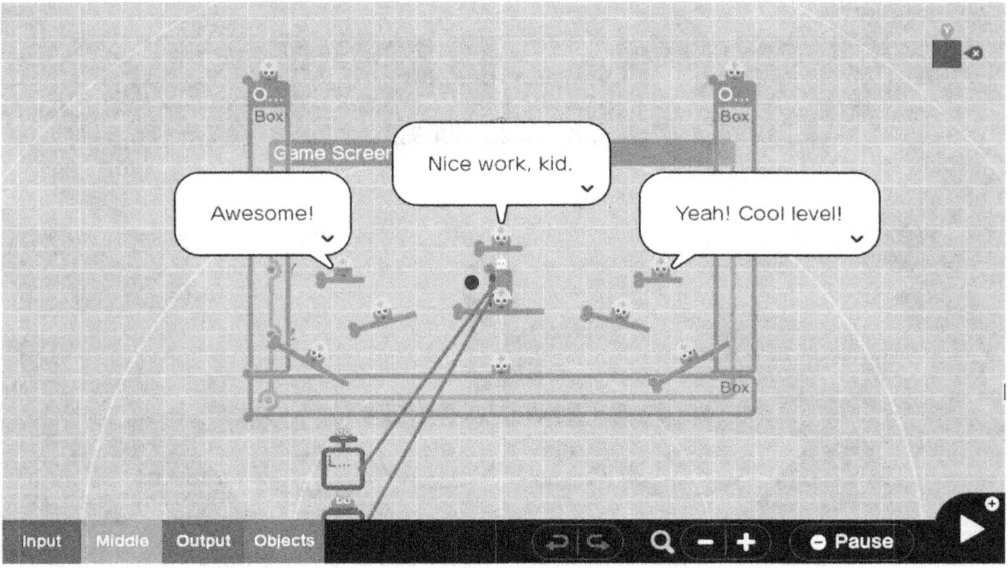

If you've ever dreamed of becoming a game developer, this is the title for you. It's made by Nintendo itself, and it feels like a next step for gamers who love creation game series Super Mario Maker.

That's because, instead of just building levels and experimenting with ideas, Game Builder Garage gives you proper coding lessons. It's been smartly made, too. Instructions are well explained, and to stop things getting too complicated you can give jobs and functions to little characters called Nodon. They help you build out your game worlds.

After each lesson, you can test yourself by making seven preset games. These include a multiplayer tag title, a motion-controlled arcade experience and even a 3D racer. You can also just go into a Sandbox mode and build ideas from scratch, as well as share your creations with friends. You can even collaborate with friends on the same idea.

As a result, this is a great game for all you creative types who are certain they can make the best game ever.

Ghosts 'n Goblins: Resurrection

Age Range = Older | **Local Multiplayer** = Yes
Difficulty = Hard | **Genre** = Platformer

Way back in the eighties there was a legendary platformer called Ghosts 'n Goblins. It was notorious for being very challenging, yet lots of fun. And its creepy, Halloween-like setting made it a favourite all around the world. In 2021, suddenly the series is back.

Despite the shinny new visuals, the game keeps very true to the original series. It's still a sidescrolling platformer, and the hero still has his quirky movements as he jumps, throws spears and uses other weapons, as well as getting crazy power-ups. One of these, for example, turns all the enemies on the screen into toads!

This is not a remake, but is a new game with new levels and boss battles to experience. But it's still tough. The fact that enemies can come at you from any direction all the time offers an old-school challenge, if you're up for it.

Goosebumps: Dead of Night

Age Range = Older | **Local Multiplayer** = No
Difficulty = Hard | **Genre** = Horror

If you're a fan of the popular Goosebumps books, then this first-person survival horror game could be just the right chill for your spine. Slappy the dummy has escaped from the books, and you need to get him back into its pages before thing go very bad indeed.

Unfortunately, a lot of the pages have gone missing and in doing so, other classic creatures have made their escape, too. Think of the Lawn Gnomes, the Werewolf of Fever Swamp and Murder the Clown. To find these pages, you need to explore spooky environments, hiding from monsters, solving puzzles and basically just avoid getting too scared.

At least there are some famous people in this strange world who will help you, like Nikola Tesla, Dr. Brewer and even the Goosebumps books' author, R.L. Stine.

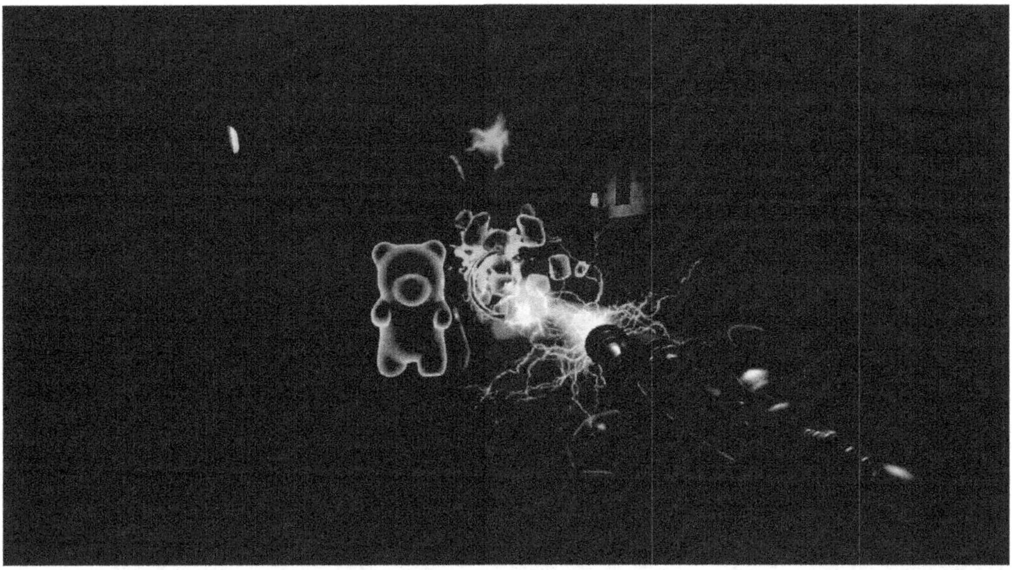

There isn't combat in this game, with the focus more on stealth and thinking up ways to distract monsters so you don't get caught. And while the visuals aren't great, if you're a fan of the books there's plenty you'll recognise. Just be warned, it's definitely for older kids as some of the moments can get quite scary.

HADES

Age Range = Older | **Local Multiplayer** = No
Difficulty = Medium | **Genre** = Roguelite

Imagine you are Zagreus — son of the Greek god Hades, king of the underworld — and you want to run away from home. Not easy right? But that's your goal in Hades, which means you're going to have to battle your way out of hell.

Story is the big surprise in this roguelite, as this genre has always struggled to make each run exist within an always progressing narrative. Yet Supergiant Games, the same studio that made Bastion and Transistor (both equally excellent Switch games), has done it successfully here.

As you fight your way through hell, you'll do so against an eclectic range of bad guys, but you'll meet many more and form relationships with some of the great names from Greek mythology.

Roguelites are always about replaying randomly generated levels repeatedly, but rarely does the cast of characters remember all your past runs. They're a fun, if strange, mob to meet, and part of the

reason while you'll happily keep making runs through hell to escape to the mortal realm.

You'll also find yourself armed with godly powers that not only get better and expand with each run you do, but can be combined in ever more exciting ways. The deep combat, involving six melee weapons with four variants each, ranged magic casting attacks and a strategic dash to help get you into advantageous positions, is a lot of fun.

With its engaging story, that's filled with cheeky dialogue, amazing visuals and persistent RPG element that ensures you're always improving, Hades has established itself as one of the great modern roguelites.

Well worth a play!

Hot Wheels: Unleashed

Age Range = All | **Local Multiplayer** = Yes
Difficulty = Medium | **Genre** = Racing

This is one of the best kart racers in years! It's based on Hot Wheels after all, the famous toy car brand I'm sure you're familiar with. Plus, it's being developed by Milestone, a genuine master of the racing genre who also made the WRC, Ride, MotoGP and Monster Energy Supercross series. It's a match made in heaven.

The game really brings the toys to life, too. They look amazing and they sound meaty. Smoke billows from tyres as you drift; flames flick out from exhaust pipes; cars roll over during big crashes. It's spectacular.

The cars have a familiar feel to drive: a bit like a mix between the drifting in games such as Mario Kart and the in-air controls of Rocket League. You'll have no problems getting use to it, but outside of boost plates, don't expect any power-ups.

The cars can be customised, though. In fact, you can break them right down and reassemble them using parts you've discovered in secret areas or otherwise earned. These rare builds not only give your collection of cars a unique feel, but the improved attributes can make

you faster! Oh, and you can create your own skin, even sharing your art online!

The tracks are insane, too. They're built from the same orange plastic you play with in the real world. But they are full of jumps, boosts, loops and even magnetic sections so you can drive up walls and along rooves upside down.

There are 40 official tracks, which span across six different environments. Each world looks huge as you play the game as if you are the size of a toy car. There's a skatepark, college, garage, skyscraper and more. But even better is the track editor. In it you have full control to build whatever fancy track you want, including using objects in the environment to your advantage, and adding props and stunts. It's easy to learn and creatively so much fun.

Naturally, it's especially fun sharing them with friends, or racing them together either online or in two-player splitscreen. Plus, there is a career mode to dive into that not only has you progressing through tracks and cars, but also taking on bosses.

What does this game not have?

Hyrule Warriors: Age of Calamity

Age Range = Older | **Local Multiplayer** = Yes
Difficulty = Medium | **Genre** = Action

This is the second game in the Hyrule Warriors series, which is a spin-off to The Legend of Zelda. It's quite a different experience, too. It's less of an adventure and more of a full-on action game with over-the-top crazy fight scenes where you take on hundreds of enemies at once.

If you're familiar with the Dynasty Warriors games, then you'll know what to expect.

This sequel tells the story of the Great Calamity, which is set 100 years before the events of Breath of the Wild and fans will enjoy learning more about that story.

While the map is familiar, as mentioned, the gameplay is very different. Your goal is to capture strategic points for your forces until

you control the whole battlefield. This involves not only fighting as yourself, but controlling your troops and even the divine beasts in some instances.

The character customisation, material crafting and weapon upgrades return, but you can now also cook food to gain buffs, use the paraglider and use the Sheikah Slate, the latter involved in new puzzle solving elements. Awesome!

IMMORTALS: FENYX RISING

Age Range = Older | **Local Multiplayer** = No
Difficulty = Medium | **Genre** = Adventure

We were all desperately wanting another big open-world adventure game like The Legend of Zelda: Breath of the Wild, and it arrived in the form of Immortals: Fenyx Rising. Welcome to a huge and vibrant world set in the era of Greek mythology.

You play as Fenyx, a warrior shipwrecked on a strange island populated by Greek gods. They ask you to help them defeat the evil Typhon and reclaim their land. Despite the serious story, the game has plenty of flair, allowing you to customise your character with new gear and cosmetics.

You'll level-up, too, which ensures the combat and exploration gets deeper as you go along. This includes being able to glide across the land and take down huge beasts in fast-paced, real-time combat. Add plenty of puzzles to solve and wonders to see, and you have a must-play experience for adventure fans.

Jump Force

Age Range = Middle | **Local Multiplayer** = Yes
Difficulty = Medium | **Genre** = Fighting

Fans of anime TV shows have plenty of reasons to jump into this game — pun intended. It's a mash-up experience, where a host of different anime series have got together in one big fighting game. Set on Earth, a threat has come to wipe out mankind and all these fighters have come together in order to fight back.

The action will remind you straight away of the Dragon Ball fighting games that unfold in huge 3D arenas. Combat is wonderfully over-the-top, with ground and air-based attacks, and environmental destruction as the fighters face off. It's a three-on-three fighter, so as you battle your way through each stage, the fights can go for quite some time.

There is a full story mode to dive into, but there is also multiplayer, of course. As for the characters, there are 33 to choose between from 13 different universes. This includes Dragon Ball, Naruto, One Piece and Yu-Gi-Oh!

It's an incredible idea, and if you love these series, it's a must own.

Kingdom Hearts: Melody of Memory

Age Range = All | **Local Multiplayer** = Yes
Difficulty = Easy | **Genre** = Music

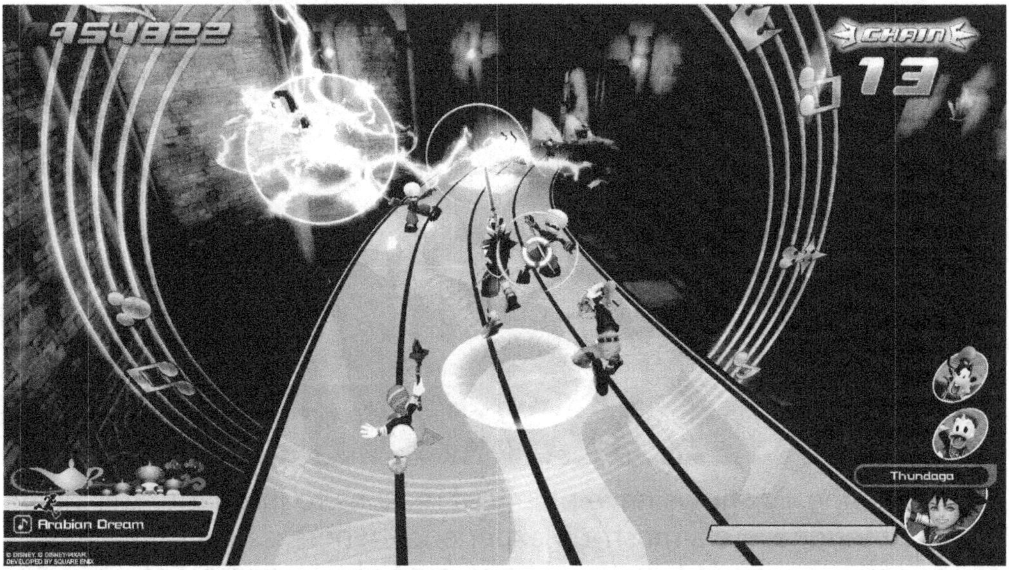

A change of pace came to beloved RPG series Kingdom Hearts in the form of Melody of Memory. This spin-off title is a rhythm-action game. You and your friends select from 20 characters and move along tracks, bashing enemies that get in your way in time with the music.

What makes it particularly cool is that the worlds are based on the same Disney universes you experience in the main Kingdom Hearts games. Plus, the songs are either from the Disney movies or the games themselves.

You've no doubt seen this kind of gameplay before — even with Guitar Hero — but it incorporates the Disney element with a sense of fun that will please fans.

KNOCKOUT CITY

Age Range = All | **Local Multiplayer** = No
Difficulty = Medium | **Genre** = Battle Royale

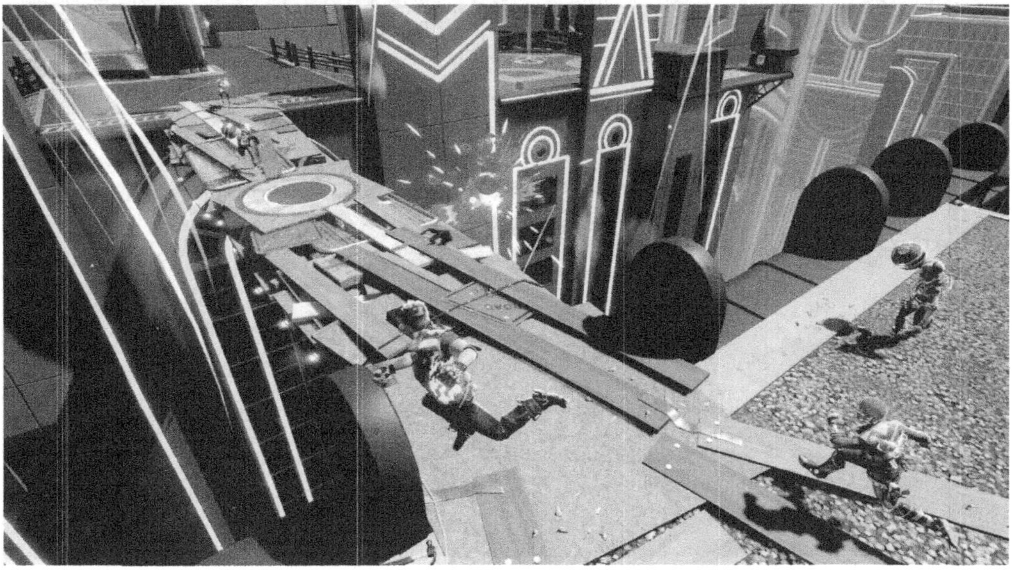

Knockout City is an online multiplayer game based on dodgeball. So instead of shooting guns, you throw balls to get a "kill." The developer has been smart enough to not make it that simple, however.

There are different types of balls that bring with them specific abilities. The Moon Ball makes you jump higher, for example, while the Bomb Ball explodes on impact. You can charge up a ball, which takes longer to throw, but turns it into a heat seeker. And you can even grab a teammate, roll them into a ball and throw them if you like.

When you're defending, you can try and catch a ball that's thrown at you, or you can tackle enemies so they drop their ball. We love the way all these gameplay mechanics make you think about different strategies. With five maps and six game modes at launch, dodgeball fans should totally check it out.

Update: By the time you read this, Knockout City may no longer be available. The developer has said it will turn the servers off in 2023.

LAST CAMPFIRE, THE

Age Range = Middle | **Local Multiplayer** = No
Difficulty = Medium | **Genre** = Puzzle Adventure

The beautiful little indie title comes from Hello Games, best know for the Joe Danger series and epic space exploration title No Man's Sky. But more specifically, it was worked on by the same creative minds from another special indie title in 2008's LostWinds. With so much indie talent behind it, no wonder it hits the mark.

The story casts you into the body of quaint hero Ember, then tasks you with finding the titular last campfire. You'll move through detailed environments and ruins from a top-down perspective, seeking campfires and the ghosts that sit by them. They will give you clues on how to find the eight lost souls you must rescue to clear a level.

Meeting a lost soul will see you transported into their last memory. Here you need to solve a logic puzzle, armed with nothing but your smarts and bag of items.

The puzzles are enjoyable and varied, making smart uses of the tools you acquire and the ability to carry objects. The difficulty is just about

perfect, too, and the game smartly opens up as you progress to bring the puzzles more into the main game world. There's no shortage of characters to meet along the way, with memorable dialogue that cleverly pulls you into this world.

Visually it's a treat and the soundtrack is great, too. I love polished, memorable indies like The Last Campfire, which sit under that 10-hour mark. They're great for the whole family.

Last Kids on Earth and the Staff of Doom, The

Age Range = All | **Local Multiplayer** = Yes
Difficulty = Easy | **Genre** = Action

Fans of The Last Kids on Earth, be it the books or the TV show, had reason to get excited by this release. It's a top-down, co-op action-adventure game set in the same world and it features a new story, too.

The tale revolves around the beloved characters needing to find the missing pieces of the powerful Staff of Doom.

You get to play as Jack, Quint, June and Dirk, each of whom has their own abilities. Jack focuses on melee, June on ranged combat, Quint is a magician/ scientist and Dirk is the tank.

You need this Staff to fight off a new enemy called Malondre, the Queen of the Slime Monsters. She is trying to summon a huge beast called Rezzoch, the Ancient Destructor of Worlds.

As part of this journey, you get to explore the whole town of Wakefield as it's overtaken by

zombies. While most of the combat occurs on foot, you do get to drive vehicles. Plus, you find plans that help you build bigger and better weapons as you go.

You'll face off against some pretty huge enemies, too. The production quality isn't amazing, however. This is typical of tie-in games like this, keeping The Last Kids on Earth and the Staff of Doom mostly in the realm of fan service.

Legend Of Zelda: Skyward Sword HD, The

Age Range = All | **Local Multiplayer** = No
Difficulty = Medium | **Genre** = Adventure

Yes, it's another HD remake, but it's hard to complain when it's a classic like 2011's The Legend of Zelda: Skyward Sword. This was the big Zelda release for the Nintendo Wii console, so it was focused on motion-controls.

You swung your sword, used your shield, and shot your bow by replicating the actions with the controllers.

You can still play this remake with motion-controls using the Switch's Joy-Cons, and now they feel much

smoother and reactive. However, you can also play with standard buttons, whereby the analogue stick controls sword swings.

The game is an origin story, detailing the creation of the Master Sword and the kingdom of Hyrule. It occurs in an era when Link lives on a floating island among the clouds. You can fly on the back of a giant bird called a Loftwing to get between areas, or plummet to the surface below in your pursuit of the kidnapped Zelda. The storytelling is very text heavy, so be warned, and the visuals are dated. But it's still an epic adventure.

Lego Super Mario and Super Luigi

Age Range = All | **Local Multiplayer** = Yes
Difficulty = Easy | **Genre** = Toy

No, it's not a new video game. It's actual new Lego set, but one with a difference. Beginning with the starter pack and then branching out through various additional packs, you can build your own Super Mario level out of Lego.

What's cool is that the main piece is an actual Mario character powered by a battery. This allows it to make classic sounds from the games and even show different things on the little screen in its tummy that change depending on what block you sit him on. It's a really neat idea and does a great job of bringing the mighty Mario into the real world.

A year or so after the Lego Super Mario kit landed, Lego Luigi joined

the fun. Its starter course has a very different feel to it than the original Mario starter course, but I still really like it. It's great fun building a platformer with real Lego. Plus, Luigi comes with a whole bunch of different sounds and reactions when he moves about his world.

There are new enemies to come across, too, and you can team up with Mario if you've got his starter pack as well. They have fun interactions with other as you play.

I did a video showing off what both kits look like that you can watch, just scan the QR code below.

Let's Sing 2022

Age Range = All | **Local Multiplayer** = Yes
Difficulty = Easy | **Genre** = Karaoke

Nothing beats a good singing game, and the Let's Sing series is the best. You get a couple of friends together and test yourself by straining your vocal cords and busting your lungs to some of the greatest songs of all time.

If you're like me, you'll want to build up your confidence by playing solo first. The main Legend game mode sees you battle through almost 20 challenges and then face off in a final battle against other artists trying to top the charts. Once complete, you can start to test yourself against up to eight friends in a range of great modes.

There are a whopping eight modes, and while they're all good, I do have some favourites. Mix Tape allows you to create your own mix of songs to sing with a playlist that never repeats. Feat mode allows you to pair up with a friend to sing together for higher scores. And Let's Party sees eight players split into two teams so they can do battle across random modes.

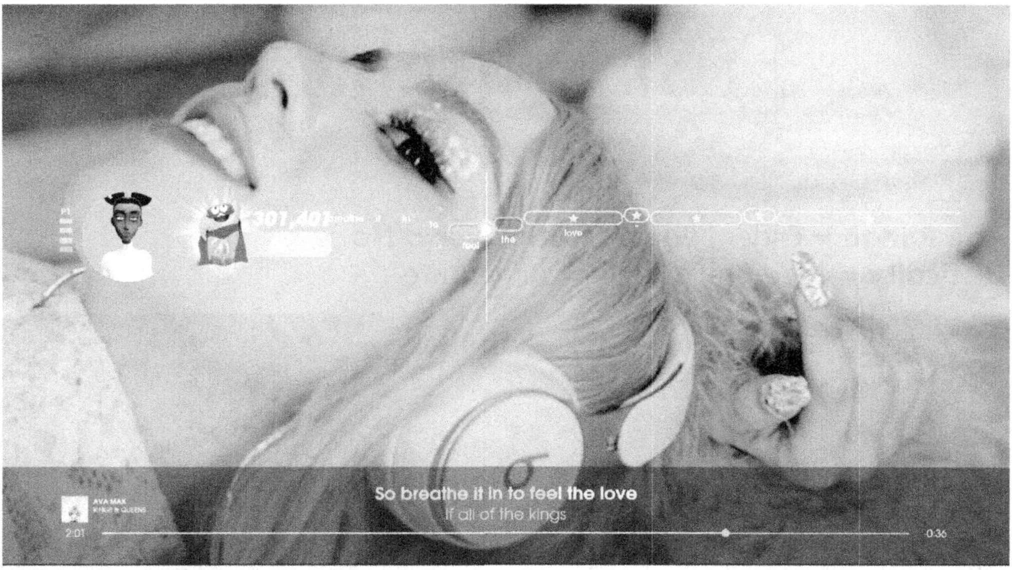

What's particularly cool with Let's Sing is that your friends don't need to have a microphone to play. There is a smartphone app that turns your phone into a microphone. This allows for you to play with lots of friends easily — it's a neat idea.

As you may have guessed, the game is all about holding those notes and delivering great vocals with the right timing, with the game scoring you points based on how well you go. As such, the track list is always a big deal. There's 30 available with Let's Sing 2022 and it's a fantastic mix of new and old songs from some of the greatest musicians of all time. (For those interested in the 2023 version, it brings an Australian and NZ focus to the song list.)

Let's Sing is the perfect way to get the laughs flowing and the good times rolling. You might even discover you're a star.

Our Top 5 Songs

1. Ariana Grande — Positions
2. Billie Eilish — Everything I Wanted
3. Lady Gaga — Stupid Love
4. Jax Jones feat. RAYE — You Don't Know Me
5. Backstreet Boys — Everybody (Backstreet's Back)

Lost in Random

Age Range = Older | **Local Multiplayer** = No
Difficulty = Medium | **Genre** = Adventure

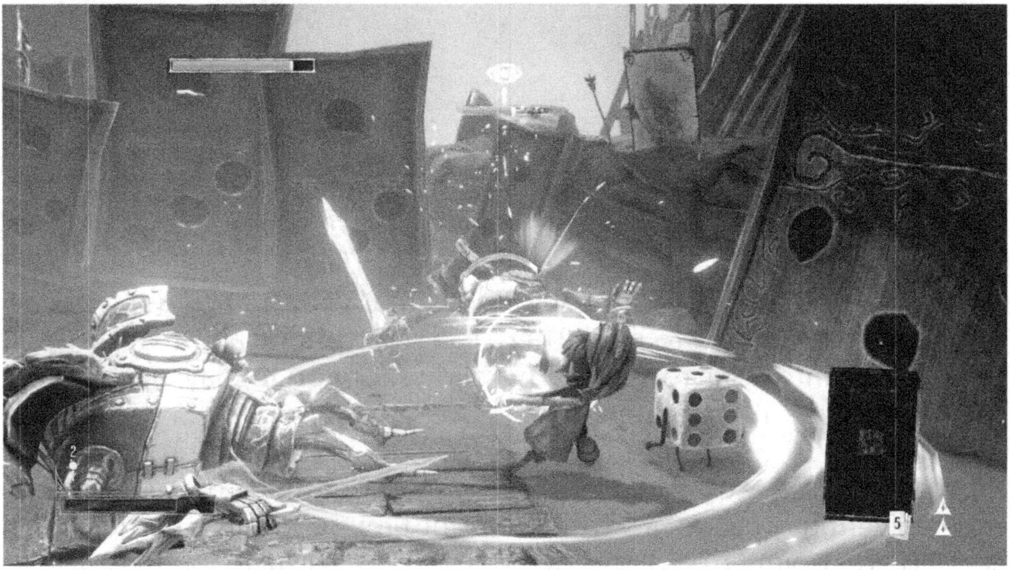

It's time to get wonderful and weird in this spectacular new adventure game. Very few worlds are as detailed and gorgeous as this one, but also filled with so many unique characters. It's like Alice in Wonderland meets Coco meets Nightmare Before Christmas.

The world is called Random, which is like a living board game. The fate of its people is decided by the roll of a dice and various game rules. You play Even, who sets out to rescue her twin sister Odd, after she is kidnapped by the Queen of Random. And you do so with the help of Dicey; a dice that has come to life.

So much of the fun comes from just exploring and meeting people. Especially as each realm feels so different. The combat is also unique. You fight with a slingshot, firing at enemies to knock crystals from their bodies. This unlock cards from your deck, as well as fuelling up Dicey for another roll. When you roll, you play these cards, which applies perks. It's a neat idea, and while the AI isn't smart enough to make the most of it, that shouldn't stop you from giving it a go.

Mario Golf: Super Rush

Age Range = All | **Local Multiplayer** = Yes
Difficulty = Easy | **Genre** = Sports

When you've got a couple of friends around on a rainy day and you're looking for something fun to play, it's hard to beat Mario's sport games. Mario Golf doesn't veer far from the formula we know and love. Including a big cast of 16 Mushroom Kingdom characters with unique special powers and moves.

It's obviously not a simulation, with simple button controls anyone can master. But you still need to think about things like wind and terrain, and you can do draw, spin and fade shots to get around obstacles. For an even more immersive experience, you can opt for motion-controls, swinging the Joy-Con as if it's a club.

What we really love about this game is the quirky four-player modes. Speed Golf has everyone teeing off at once and running to each shot; dashing and shoving each other out of the way. There's also Battle Golf, which is a battle royale style game that unfolds in a big arena. So, there's a lot of value here for sport fans.

Mario Kart Live: Home Circuit

Age Range = All | **Local Multiplayer** = Yes
Difficulty = Easy | **Genre** = Racing

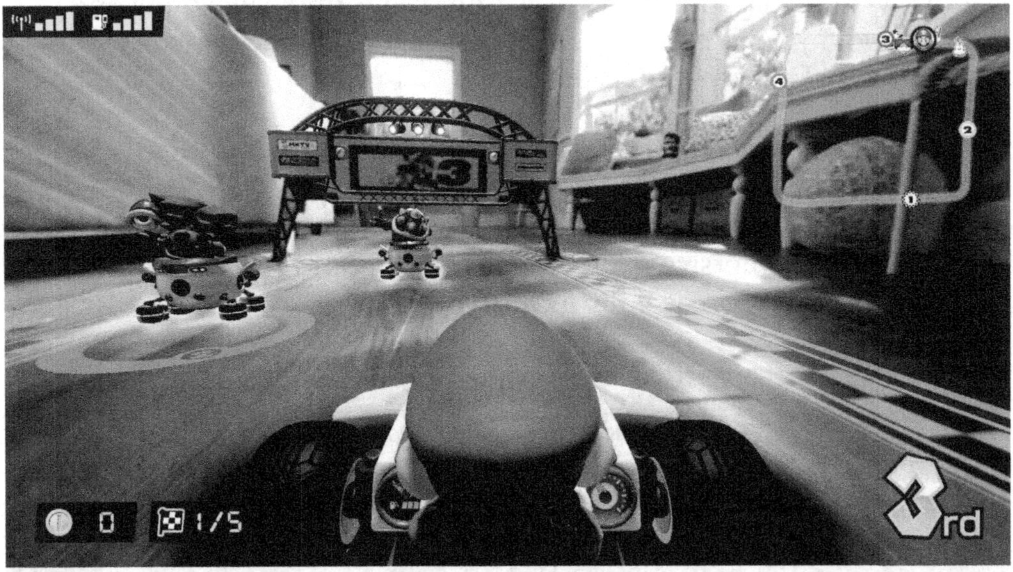

Yet again, the magicians at Nintendo have come up with a new way to play video games using the Switch console. This time, it's augmented reality. So, it's a bit like Pokémon Go, although this time it involves racing karts.

This is how it works: when you buy the game, you get an actual toy version of Mario or Luigi sitting in his kart and then you get a bunch of augmented reality cards that represent different parts of a track. You then lay these cards around your home to build your own track, adding things like items and boosts in key spots.

Once you've built your track, you use the Nintendo Switch to remote control the kart as you race around the track you just made. The screen giving you a view from behind the driver's head.

The view from the kart can be seen on the screen and AI opponents are added, so it totally works to make it feel like you are racing in your house. You can even race against friends in local multiplayer. If you really get into it, you can create trackside items out of objects by using other toys, books, cups and so forth. It's kind of mind-blowing.

In late 2021, a 2.0 update arrived bringing more content. The free update added splitscreen multiplayer, a four-player Relay race mode, three new tracks — Windmill Meadows, Music Broadway and King Boo's Courtyard — as well as two new items, Luigi's Poltergust and the Spooky Horn.

Mario Party Superstars

Age Range = All | **Local Multiplayer** = Yes
Difficulty = Easy | **Genre** = Party

If you love getting some friends around for multiplayer chaos, then Mario Party is a winner. Especially Mario Party Superstars, as it's a "best of" collection from all the previous titles.

Mario Party is a board game brought to life. You roll dice and move about a board with branching paths and obstacles, competing for stars. When you land on a tile, something will happen, usually in the form of a minigame. This pits you and the three other players against each in fast-paced, fun, competitive play.

There's only five board, but they are all classics from the N64 era redone with shiny new graphics. But at least there are 100 minigames, and they are the best from across the series, so they're all good. Plus, you can play them in solo or team-based modes, or via online play.

If you played the previous Switch game in the series — 2018's Super Mario Party — you'll be happy to know you can now use any kind of controller and set your own game rules, too.

Marvel's Guardians of the Galaxy

Age Range = Middle | **Local Multiplayer** = No
Difficulty = Medium | **Genre** = Action

There have certainly been some good superhero games coming out lately — namely Marvel's Spider-Man and Marvel's The Avengers — and another one has landed with Marvel's Guardians of the Galaxy.

It's made by the guys and girls behind Marvel's The Avengers, and you'll be happy to know the great visuals, action setpieces and fast combat of that game can be found here, too. There are some key differences, however.

You play only as Star-Lord, with the AI controlling Gamora, Rocket Raccoon, Groot and Drax the Destroyer. While it's a shame that a friend can't play them in co-op, you can issue the AI commands.

It takes a while to get used to this style of play, but the controls are easy enough to master and once you understand how it works, there's plenty of depth to the strategies you can use in combat. In fact, a big part of the fun is giving your crew a motivational speech, then trying to chain together their unique abilities to create devastating attacks.

Just be warned, your teammates may not always agree with your plans!

The story sees the Guardians trying to fix a little mistake they made in pursuit of making some money: a mistake that could bring about the end of the universe. It's cool that the story isn't linear, with branching paths and dialogue trees. And indeed, just listening to their banter is fun.

You don't have to be a fan of the movie or tcomics to enjoy Marvel's Guardians of the Galaxy, but it does help.

Marsupilami Hoobadventure

Age Range = All | **Local Multiplayer** = No
Difficulty = Easy | **Genre** = Platformer

While the name Marsupilami doesn't mean much outside of Europe, in places like Belgium, it's a big deal. Marsupilami started as a comic way back in the 1950s and became very popular. Now it's a game.

The setting is the mythical, tropical land of Palombia. Our three Marsupilami heroes — called Punch, Twister and Hope — are happily living the good life when things go bad. They find an ancient sarcophagus lying on the beach and when they open it, a strange ghost emerges.

This curses all the animals in Palombia except the Marsupilami. As such, your mission is to explore the land, find the ghost and reverse the curse. It's the kind of classic story we're used to seeing in a 2.5D platformer, and even adventure, genre. And indeed, Marsupilami Hoobadventure has the same kind of cheerful characters, colours and vibe of hits like Super Mario, Banjo-Kazooie, Ty the Tasmanian Tiger and Yoola-Laylee. If you like those kinds of games, you'll fall in love with the look of Marsupilami straight away.

The gameplay also recalls classic of the genre. You'll be jumping your way across platforms and through obstacle filled levels looking for collectables and fighting off bad guys. All the classic moves you'd expect are here, such as doing ground stomps, wall jumps and dash rolls (think Sonic).

The Marsupilami also have these long tails that can be used to grapple anchor points in the world to reach higher locations.

The level design reminds us quite a bit of Sonic the Hedgehog. Perhaps that is because you use your dash roll a lot of the time. But you can expect a lot of varied environments across the three different worlds you explore. Think jungles, abandoned temples, coastal cities — that kind of thing.

Each section is packed with lots to see and quirky critters to get past. You'll also come across bigger boss battles, too.

There's no multiplayer mode in this one; it's all about the story adventure. However, there is an online time attack mode that challenges you to speed run levels.

Metroid Dread

Age Range = Older | **Local Multiplayer** = No
Difficulty = Hard | **Genre** = Metroidvania

The Metroid series, starring bounty hunter Samus, is one of gaming's most beloved franchises. In fact, it was so influential when it first came out as a non-linear platformer, they named a genre after it. It's called a Metroidvania, no doubt you've heard of it.

While the main games in the series have branched off into full 3D action territory, Metroid Dread returns to the classic sidescrolling gameplay of the original games. And boy is it still fun!

Samus once again finds herself on an alien planet, this time called ZDR. A robot army is the main threat this time around, and

Samus has been given a stack of new abilities to help her survive. She can slide, cling to blue surfaces, free aim and use melee attacks. Plus, she can use stealth to evade serious threats. This includes a Phantom Cloak that camouflages her, even if it also slows her down.

These join classic abilities like rolling into a ball, and it's all upgradeable. There's an increased sense of scale, with some huge bosses, too. And more tension than previous games. As we all await for the arrival of Metroid Prime 4, this is a fantastic way to get a taste of Samus' amazing gameplay. We really like it!

Miitopia

Age Range = All | **Local Multiplayer** = Yes
Difficulty = Easy | **Genre** = JRPG

Miitopia is a JRPG that stars Mii characters instead of regular game heroes. It's an unusual twist for this genre because RPGs are usually so focused on big over-the-top characters.

But because the story and gameplay are kept so light-hearted and simple, it works well. Plus, because it stars a whole bunch of Mii characters, you can deeply customise their appearance.

Also unusual in this game is the relationship system; you need to constantly talk to other characters — and even animals like horses. If you have fun with them, they'll help you more in battle. But if you irritate them, they may choose to fight you!

The battles themselves are turn-based, kind of like the Pokémon games. While the story is bizarre; it's about a Dark Lord that has come to Miitopia and stolen people's faces and stuck them on monsters. What the?! So, your goal is to defeat the monsters to get back the people's faces, grabbing loot and levelling-up stats as you go.

Monster Hunter Rise

Age Range = Older | **Local Multiplayer** = Yes
Difficulty = Hard | **Genre** = Action-RPG

The epic action-RPG series Monster Hunter is frequently a Switch launch exclusive nowadays. It's a huge win for Nintendo fans, as this is an engrossing series. Rise is not a spin-off — for which the series is famous — but the next mainline instalment following 2018's Monster Hunter: World.

This series is all about exploring a huge open world as you hunt down epic monsters. You need to best them in combat in order to loot their remains for body parts that can help you craft better gear. The better your gear, the bigger the monster you can hunt when you next leave a city and head into the wilds.

What's particularly cool is that you can play this game with friends in co-op!

New to the series with Monster Hunter Rise, besides fresh monsters of course, is a world map more focused on vertical play. The new Wirebug tool allows you to grapple up to high areas and swing across gaps. It also adds a variation to the 14 different weapon types, bringing more strategy to combos in battle.

You also now explore with cat and dog companion pets, the latter able to ride up cliffs and into battle. Yes, it's just more Monster Hunter in many ways as it's not a series that evolves a lot with each entry, but that core gameplay loop is still so very cool.

Monster Hunter Stories 2: Wings of Ruin

Age Range = Middle | **Local Multiplayer** = Yes
Difficulty = Medium | **Genre** = Action-RPG

Even if you hadn't read the previous game review, we're sure you know about the epic action-RPG series Monster Hunter. Its realistic medieval visuals and epic real-time battles have made it one of gaming's most beloved franchises.

Well, there's also a spin-off series called Stories, which is quite different. It is more story focused — der! — with a cartoon anime style. It also features turn-based battles more like a Pokémon game.

While some characters return from the first Stories game, there is a new tale to be found here that begins with a strange light that is sending monsters crazy.

This includes the Razewing Ratha, which could potentially destroy the entire world.

There's much more strategy in the battles this time around, as you choose weapon types and attacks to better suit the enemy you're facing. And we love that a friend can still join in online co-op.

Monster collection has also changed. Now you can ride your monster into the depths of dens, defeating beasts so you can capture eggs. You can then hatch these eggs and then transfer genes between monsters to create your own unique beasts. Very cool.

Basically, it's like Monster Hunter meets the Pokémon series, which is as rad as it sounds.

MotoGP 22

Age Range = Middle | **Local Multiplayer** = No
Difficulty = Hard | **Genre** = Racing

MotoGP 22 is the official simulation of the world's premiere two-wheeled championship. You get access to the full 2022 season, and when you add in all the historical riders, that works out to over 20 tracks and 120 riders.

You can free play, do a full season and race online, plus the managerial career is back, where you own an entire team that you're trying to bring to championship glory. But it's the new additions we really love.

While the feel of the bikes has always been great, the fact it's a simulation means it can be challenging to master. So, the addition of a MotoGP Academy mode, a better tutorial experience and adaptive difficulty makes it much easier for newcomers.

Advanced players still get improvements to the suspension, impacts of deformation and temperatures on tyres and track surfaces, and ride height customisation. Add stunning visuals and splitscreen multiplayer, and you've got the best game in the series to date.

My Universe: Puppies and Kittens

Age Range = All | **Local Multiplayer** = No
Difficulty = Easy | **Genre** = Simulation

Whether you're desperate to get your own pet or have one already, you can never get enough of cute little critters. My Universe: Puppies and Kittens is a simulation game, which means it takes a real-life experience and replicates it in a virtual world. This gives you a chance to play make believe, learning about and living the life of someone else.

In this case, someone who owns puppies and kittens from 20 different breeds.

You become a pet owner by playing different minigames. These allow you to teach, pat, feed, look after and play with your pets. Each breed is different, so you'll need to work out what it is that your adopted pet likes so you can forge a great relationship.

This earns you the "money" you need to unlock new items and equipment so you can do more tricks and activities together.

A lot of the action takes place in your home, but you can also explore the neighbourhood. Whether you're walking to the dog park or the shops, you'll encounter other creatures for your pet to befriend, as well as hunting down treasures and talking to other owners.

To be honest, I found this game to be tediously slow and the interactions with the pets frustrating to control. I didn't rate it at all. However, my eight-year-old daughter loves it. And considering that we have kids front of mind in this book, I thought I should include it.

Need for Speed: Hot Pursuit Remastered

Age Range = Middle | **Local Multiplayer** = No
Difficulty = Medium | **Genre** = Racing

There's was no new Need for Speed game in 2021, so instead famed series developer EA dusted off one of its earlier classics. It's a great chance for newcomers and nostalgia chases to enjoy its thrills as this 2021 entry is one of the best entries in this long-running series.

This remastered version doesn't add a whole lot. There are better visuals, more environment detail and a new garage mode to help show off your cars. The same great game with a fresh coat of paint.

So, what made this game great? Being able to play as either the cops or the criminals in epic, over-the-top car chases dominated by fast speeds and big crashes. And then unlocking better cars the further you ventured through the various events. It also has an ever-present multiplayer experience where you're constantly trying to beat the results of your friends.

Nerf: Legends

Age Range = Middle | **Local Multiplayer** = Yes
Difficulty = Medium | **Genre** = FPS

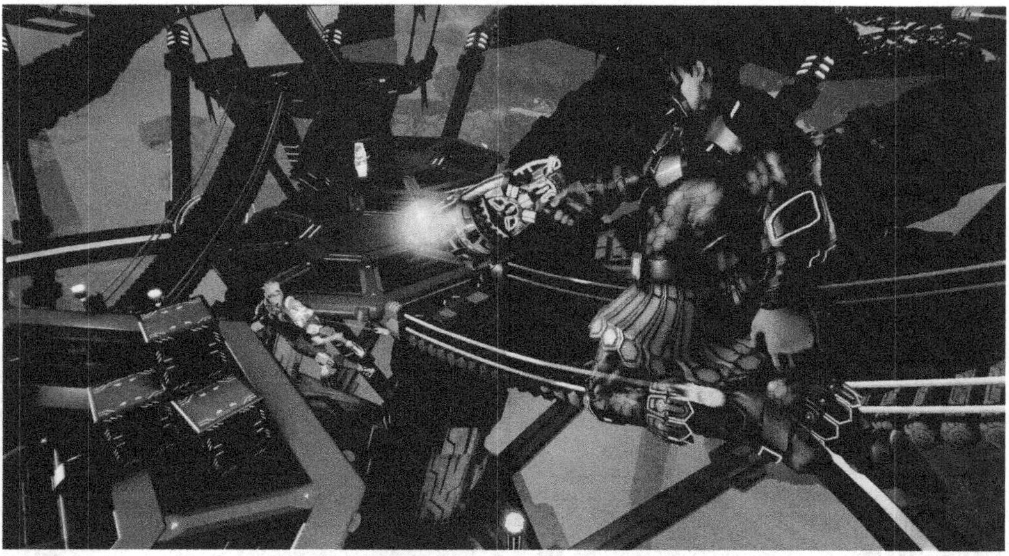

Talk about a match made in heaven. The awesome Nerf toys — a giant catalogue of weapons that fire foam bullets across your house, at your siblings and over your pets — are perfect for a game conversion. It's almost like a real-life video game playing with Nerf guns in your home, you just don't get a cool sci-fi setting.

Plus, you must pick up all those darn bullets!

As you may have guessed, Nerf: Legends is a kid-friendly first-person shooter starring the Nerf toys. It's set in a science-fiction world, filled with big 3D arenas and levels to battle through. At first sight, it feels like a mix of Halo and Fortnite, which can only be a good thing, right?

The game features a full single player campaign to battle through. You'll need to make your way past armies of varied robot enemies, as well as the bosses who control them. You can expect 19 different locations, too. And it's not all fighting, as you will come across puzzles that can only be solved with the right kind of shots.

But for many, it will be the eight-player online multiplayer experience where they'll spend most of their time. As well as free-for-all, there are 4v4 team-based matches as well. And we like that you can play cross-platform, which should ensure a healthy player base.

Naturally you can create and customise your own character, and even personalise the blasters as well. You do this with perks that you unlock as you play through the game.

Moment-to-moment gameplay is really fast-paced. As well as shooting and swapping weapons, you have a melee attack and a shield. There

are powerups to find as well. For example, magnetic pull darts, push darts, seeker darts and slow darts. Plus, you can pull off trick shots by nailing a great frag while jumping through the air or doing something similarly cool.

But, the stars of the game are the weapons, based as they are on the real-world toys. At launch, there were 14 Nerf blasters from the real-world that have been lovingly recreated in game. They're listed below. They span the Mega, Ultra and Elite lines. It's cool seeing them in action, especially when it's a Nerf blaster you have used in real life.

The first-person shooter genre is one of our favourites, but most of the games are too violent for kids. As such, it's great to see a kid-friendly game, with full online play, come out for shooter fans.

Which Nerf blasters were included at launch?

- Bulldog
- Centurion
- CycloneShock
- Delta Trooper
- Disruptor
- Dual-Strike
- The Judge
- Mega Mastodon
- ONE
- RaptorStrike
- Shockwave RD-15
- Strongarm (Elite XD)
- Titan CS-50
- Trilogy DS-15

NEW POKEMON SNAP

Age Range = All | **Local Multiplayer** = No
Difficulty = Easy | **Genre** = Adventure

Back in 1999, the first Pokémon Snap game came out and people weren't excited. Not initially, anyway. Yes, it was a new Pokémon game, but you didn't play as a traditional hero. You were just a photographer. Your job was to try and take cool photos of Pokémon in their natural habitat.

But it actually turned out to be really good fun. Now, all these years later, a sequel has arrived.

The visuals look amazing, too. You are automatically moved through these beautiful environments so you don't walk around. Instead your focus is on trying to spot Pokémon doing rare activities and then snapping a photo.

You have tricks up your sleeve to get them looking amazing, like offering food or orbs that make them glow. Once you've edited your photos to make them look extra pretty, you can share them with friends and compete online to see if you're the best photographer.

Nickelodeon All-Star Brawl

Age Range = All | **Local Multiplayer** = Yes
Difficulty = Easy | **Genre** = Fighter

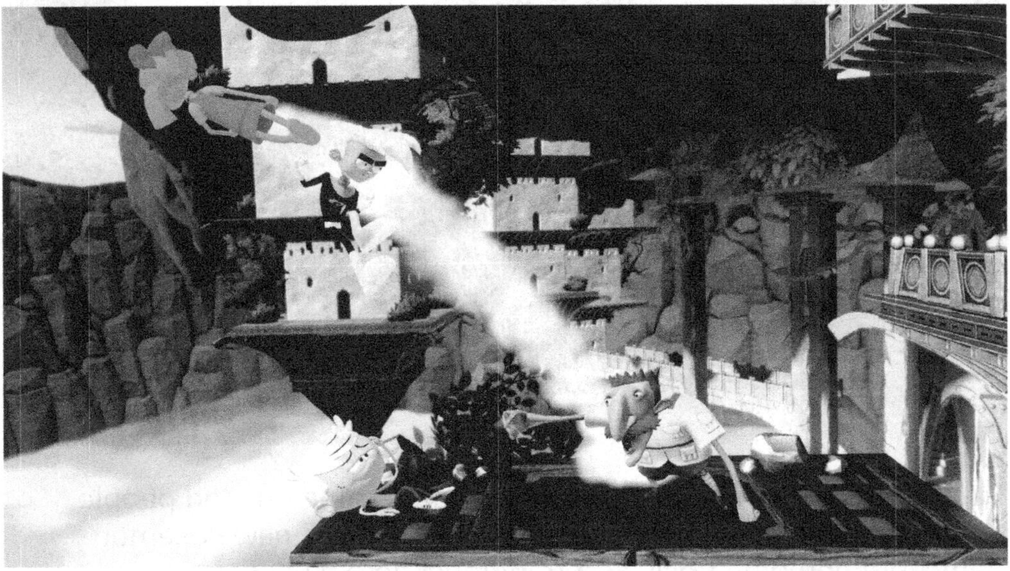

If you love games like Super Smash Bros. Ultimate or Brawlhalla, then this is a game for you. The coolest characters from across the Nickelodeon TV universe have decided they want to join in the fun, too. They're starring in their own fighting game and it's as over-the-top and amazing as you would expect.

If you have played these kinds of fighting games before, you will be immediately at home in Nickelodeon All-Star Brawl. The action unfolds in 2D battle arenas that are based on locations from across the shows. Your goal is to bash up your opponents until their damage gets high enough that you can knock them off the edge and out of the screen. All while dodging hazards in the world itself.

You can combo together light, strong and special attacks, which vary depending on how you press the buttons and sticks. You can dash through the air in eight directions, block incoming attacks and — of course — run and jump. You can grab and throw enemies, plus there are projectiles you can use, too.

One cool addition we haven't seen in a fighting game before is the strafe button. This allows you to move backwards, as in retreat from a fight, without turning around and leaving yourself vulnerable.

Overall, the combat is great and while like Smash Bros, it's definitely not the exact same! You'll be surprised by how much it changes combat by allowing every character to have an air dash.

There are not many modes, though. You a have the standard Arcade to play through in single player, or you can fight it our with up to four friends online or offline. There's also a quirky but cool Sports Mode, which brings in a Rocket League element. Your goal isn't to defeat opponents, but to get a ball in the back of the net. However, there are many kinds of balls, each behaving in a different way.

We really like the super colourful visuals. The worlds and characters look great, and the action is super-fast. It's also nice hearing familiar tunes from the TV shows in the background as you play. I do wish there were more items and objects to pick up and use in battles, but that doesn't stop the gameplay from being a lot of fun.

List of Base Fighters (and their show)

- Oblina (Aaahh!!! Real Monsters)
- Aang (Avatar: The Last Airbender)
- Toph Beifong (Avatar: The Last Airbender)
- CatDog (CatDog)
- Danny Phantom (Danny Phantom)
- Helga Pataki (Hey Arnold!)
- Zim (Invader Zim)
- Korra (The Legend of Korra)
- Lincoln Loud (The Loud House)
- Lucy Loud (The Loud House)
- Ren & Stimpy (Ren & Stimpy)
- Powdered Toast Man (Ren & Stimpy)
- Reptar (Rugrats)
- SpongeBob SquarePants (SpongeBob SquarePants)
- Patrick Star (SpongeBob SquarePants)
- Sandy Cheeks (SpongeBob SquarePants)
- Leonardo (TMNT)
- Michelangelo (TMNT)
- April O'Neil (TMNT)
- Nigel Thornberry (The Wild Thornberrys)

Nickelodeon Kart Racers 2: Grand Prix

Age Range = All | **Local Multiplayer** = Yes
Difficulty = Easy | **Genre** = Racing

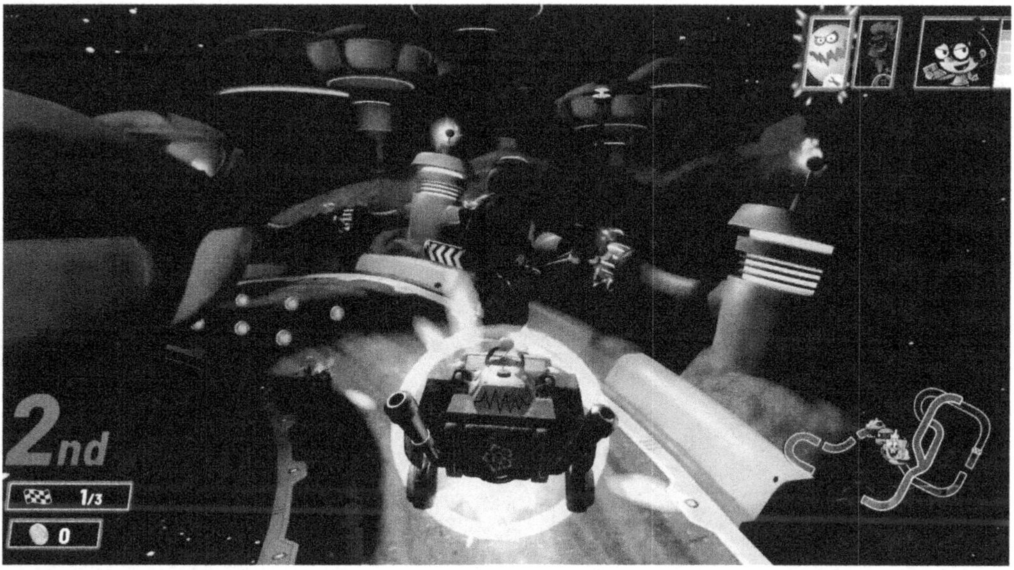

Ever since Mario Kart first came out in 1992, gamers have loved any chance to jump on the couch with their friends to race around ridiculous tracks filled with obstacles and power-ups. It's usually a great chance for us to experience a mix of our favourite heroes in the same game, too. And, of course, that is one of the features that makes this sequel to Nickelodeon Kart Racers so cool.

There's a huge roster of familiar faces from the Nickelodeon TV channel. There's more than double the characters of the last game from a much broader range of shows. Racing as each of them — in their own little karts — is awesome. Plus, there are stacks of visual customisations you can unlock for each of the karts to add personality. This are also part upgrades.

As you'd hope, there's four-player splitscreen to enjoy with your friends. But this time around there is also an eight-player online mode, too. This joins your other typical kart racing modes like Cups, Time Trials and Battles.

In all there is a healthy 28 circuits to race on, as well as two arenas to battle in. All of which feature locations you will recognise from the various Nickelodeon shows.

There's classic kart racing to be had here. The tracks look spectacular thanks to improved visuals and they're filled with boosts and power-ups that you can unleash to try and get an advantage mid-race. You can also fill up your slime bar, which brings stunts and cool tricks into play when you launch off jumps. It should come as no surprise that there is plenty of slime to watch out for as well.

The first Nickelodeon Kart Racers title was solid, but this sequel really goes a lot bigger. There's been a lot of great improvements to the gameplay, there's stacks more characters to try out and some great multiplayer experiences to enjoy.

List of Playable Base Characters

There are 30 base characters available to race in Nickelodeon Kart Racers 2. There's an additional 70 companion characters, too. You don't race as these side characters, but instead collect them for your pit crew, giving your kart certain buffs. Here are you base drivers:

- Tommy Pickles (Rugrats)
- Chuckie Finster (Rugrats)
- Angelica Pickles (Rugrats)
- Reptar (Rugrats)
- Ren Höek (Ren & Stimpy)
- Stimpy J. Cat (Ren & Stimpy)
- Rocko Rama (Rocko's Modern Life)
- Heffer Wolfe (Rocko's Modern Life)
- Arnold Shortman (Hey Arnold!)
- Gerald Johanssen (Hey Arnold!)
- Helga Pataki (Hey Arnold!)
- CatDog (CatDog)
- SpongeBob SquarePants (SpongeBob SquarePants)
- Patrick Star (SpongeBob SquarePants)
- Squidward Tentacles (SpongeBob SquarePants)
- Sandy Cheeks (SpongeBob SquarePants)
- Zim (Invader Zim)
- GIR (Invader Zim)
- Danny Phantom (Danny Phantom)
- Aang (Avatar: The Last Airbender)
- Korra (The Legend of Korra)
- Leonardo (TMNT)
- Donatello (TMNT)
- Michelangelo (TMNT)
- Raphael (TMNT)
- Shredder (TMNT)
- Lincoln Loud (The Loud House)
- Lucy Loud (The Loud House)
- Clyde McBride (The Loud House)
- JoJo Siwa

NINJALA

Age Range = All | **Local Multiplayer** = No
Difficulty = Medium | **Genre** = Fighter

This unusual Switch exclusive is full of crazy, but awesome, ideas. For example, Ninjala is the name of tournament that's run by the World Ninja Association. If you have the DNA of a ninja, all you have to do to enter is chew their special bubble gum and you will suddenly master all the skills of ninjutsu. If only that was true in real life!

The focus is on online battles for eight players, either team-based or in solo mode. The weirdness carries across to the melee combat, where you can hide in the map as an object and blow bubbles to get special abilities like air-dashes and charges.

This joins more standard actions like double-jumps and wall-runs, but even the size of your weapon can be increased by defeating drones that pop-up mid-battle.

It all plays out like a 3D version of Super Smash Bros and while it's got Japanese quirkiness everywhere, it's not short on laughs and action.

Olympic Games Tokyo 2020 - The Official Video Game

Age Range = All | **Local Multiplayer** = Yes
Difficulty = Easy | **Genre** = Sports

After a long delay thanks to COVID, the 2020 Olympics finally happening in Tokyo and we finally got its tie-in video game. In short, as well as watching all your sporting heroes on TV, you can also go for gold yourself.

Despite being the official game, the developer has taken a very arcade-like approach to the action. It's not a serious simulation and is designed so anyone can pick up the controller and play with ease.

There are even 50 different costumes you can wear, dressing up in things as silly as pirate outfits and astronaut suits.

There are 18 sports in total you can play through, either together on the same couch or online with up to eight people. Expect tennis, baseball, soccer, rock climbing, rugby, ping pong, running, swimming, basketball, long hump, hammer throw, boxing, BMX and more. So, there's a lot of variety.

The visuals are pretty basic and it's a shame they haven't taken the sports a bit more seriously, but it's still a fun way to get involved with the Olympics at home.

Ori: The Collection

Age Range = Middle | **Local Multiplayer** = No
Difficulty = Medium | **Genre** = Platformer

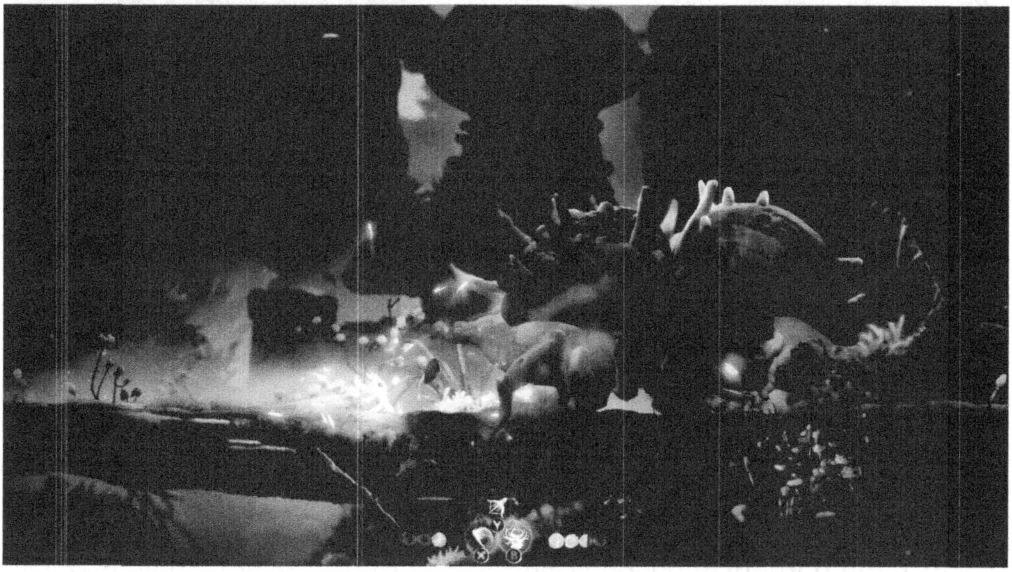

In 2015, Xbox surprised us all with atmospheric, exploratory platformer, Ori and the Blind Forest. So it was with some surprise that Nintendo's rival in the console space released the game on the Switch.

The game stands out for its gorgeous visuals, great ability progression, incredible atmosphere and smart level design. The controls work great, and there is a spiritual wonder to the story and the world that captures your imagination.

The difficulty can spike suddenly here and there, and the melee combat is a bit ineffectual compared to your abilities, but these are small gripes in the grander scheme of things. Ultimately it has indie charm with AAA polish.

Shortly after Ori and the Blind Forest, Xbox followed up this move by also bringing the game's 2020 follow-up to the Switch as well. This sequel, Will

of the Wisps, ramps up the visuals, refines the gameplay and dives deeper into the lore of this fascinating world.

As the spirit Ori, you get to venture out beyond the forest of the first game on a mission to uncover the truth about the Lost Ones and to discover Ori's role in the world's destiny.

In truth, the gameplay hasn't changed too much. As you solve puzzles to make your way further through the world, you'll get a chance to learn new abilities. This gives you access to areas you previously couldn't reach, meaning you're always finding places you know you'll be able to come back to and enjoy later.

Those who played the first game will be happy to know there's a new autosave feature as well as a simpler upgrade tree. Plus, Ori is even more agile, with fast melee and ranged attacks that help keep him one step ahead of the weird and wonderful beasts that fill every level.

The games can be purchases separately, but you also get them both in a Collection pack, which is definitely worth considering.

Override 2: Super Mech League

Age Range = Middle | **Local Multiplayer** = Yes
Difficulty = Hard | **Genre** = Fighting

There's nothing particularly complex about Override 2, but it still manages to be one of the more addictive fighting games around. Why? Because being a giant mech robot fighting other mech robots and watching whole cities get destroyed in the process is a lot of fun.

There's 20 customisable mechs in the base game, and as you might expect there are differences in their ultimate moves, weapons and abilities, giving you a chance to master a range of fight styles. Especially as you can combo and charge them up in different ways.

New in this sequel is environment hazards to avoid or lure enemies into. Think lava and geysers, or platforms that can give you a strategic advantage. There's also a long career mode to dive into. But we most enjoy the multiplayer, which includes four-player local as well as online play. There is a range of multiplayer modes, too.

PAPER MARIO: THE ORIGAMI KING

Age Range = All | **Local Multiplayer** = Yes
Difficulty = Easy | **Genre** = Platformer RPG

Announced and then released within a month — somewhat typical of Nintendo nowadays — the arrival of the sixth Paper Mario game was a pleasant surprise for Switch owners.

If you're not familiar with the Paper Mario series, it's one of the more inventive of the many Mario spin-off games. As the name suggests, the world and characters are made of paper.

That idea lends itself into your abilities and the level design in ways that are full of fun surprises.

Time around the world is under attack from the Origami King, who is folding the world in all kinds of horrible ways. You, Bowser and a new friend, Olivia, need to unfold this threat. The visuals look incredible, and the variety in this game is truly amazing.

While the sidescrolling gameplay itself is familiar, being able to peel back bits of the world, enter turn-based battle arenas where you must line-up enemies to do maximum damage, explore open world 3D sections and even do things like drive a boat or a car, ensure this is one unique experience.

PIKMIN 3 DELUXE

Age Range = Middle | **Local Multiplayer** = Yes
Difficulty = Medium | **Genre** = Puzzle Strategy

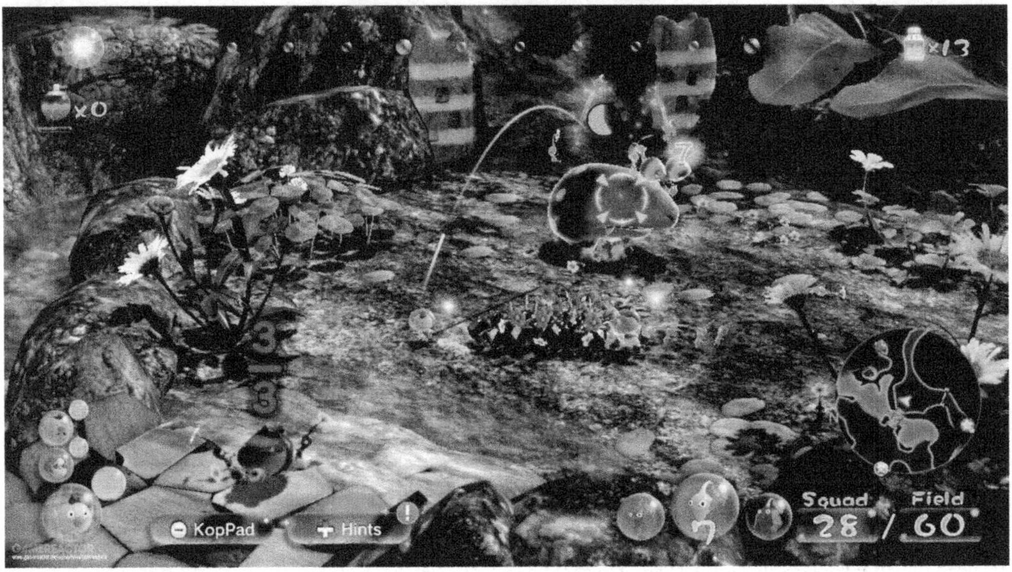

Nintendo has a long legacy of building whacky games that sit between genres. Few are more curious than the Pikmin series. It's part puzzle game, part real-time strategy and it's got a healthy sense of adventure in it, too.

In it, you play a captain who lands on the alien planet PNF-404, tasked with exploring its five different locations, getting around obstacles, defeating enemies and collecting resources. To do this you take control of an army of plant-like critters called Pikmin.

These come in five different colours, with each colour indicating what it is immune to and how it attacks.

Gameplay sees you building up your armies of Pikmin, then using their abilities to explore the world. You can split your forces, so you can have multiple parties to switch between at any given time, keeping you very active.

Plus, you view this world as if you're an inch high, and the glorious design and visuals are the perfect fodder for imaginations young and old. The smart controls help make the relatively complex gameplay easy to understand, too. This game is great brain food, offering harmless but engrossing fun for all ages.

The Deluxe edition for Switch is an upgraded port from the game that originally appeared on Wii U in 2013. It adds new prologue and epilogue story sections, all the DLC, extra difficulty modes and — best of all — cooperative play through the story mode. An excellent game!

Plants vs Zombies: Battle for Neighborville

Age Range = Middle | **Local Multiplayer** = Yes
Difficulty = Hard | **Genre** = Online Shooter

Plants vs Zombies is more than just a mobile tower defence game. There is also this fully 3D online shooter. Filled with bright colours, over-the-top attacks, strange characters and amazing maps, it's kind of like a Call of Duty game, but with the fun and silliness of Fortnite.

With the addition of six new character classes for this threequel, there are now 20 to choose from. Each fall into either an attacker, defender or support class. This allows you to play a specific role in your team.

New to the series, players of the same class can combine mid-battle to take on new forms, which is a very cool idea. We also like the hub areas, where you can meet other players and enjoy minigames away from the main online action. While the focus is on multiplayer (including local splitscreen), there is PvE gameplay as well, with quests and collectables on offer as you explore maps filled with AI enemies.

Pokemon Brilliant Diamond and Shiny Pearl

Age Range = All | **Local Multiplayer** = No
Difficulty = Medium | **Genre** = Adventure RPG

As you know, Nintendo loves a remake. Even though we have had a few exciting new entries in the Pokémon series during the Switch era, the company has been happy to reimagine some classics, too.

The original Pokémon Diamond and Pearl games came out on the handheld DS console in 2006, so this game retains that simpler top-down view of the older games. However, everything has been remade with proper 3D models and new textures, so the Japanese inspired land of Sinnoh looks a lot better.

Other additions include the sharing of XP between Pokémon after a fight, autosaves, better visualised attacks and the ability to have a critter follow you around when walking about.

The original game was already a lot of fun, and there really is a lot to do. The Contest Shows return, allowing you to show off your Pokémon to try and win awards through rhythm-based minigames. The Pokétch watch has been remade to look more modern, giving you access to apps like a drawing pad and item dowsing machine.

Hidden Machines are back, too, allowing you to use Pokémon abilities to interact with the world. Plus, the Grand Underground, with dungeons for you to explore beneath the world. It may not be a new game, but it offers more than just simple nostalgia, too.

Pokemon Unite

Age Range = Middle | **Local Multiplayer** = No
Difficulty = Medium | **Genre** = MOBA

Multiplayer Online Battle Arenas are part strategy, part action and part RPG. The general idea is to use the abilities of your hero characters — which level-up as you complete objectives and beat AI minions — to gain control of the lanes between your base and the enemy's base.

How you manage your upgrades and use your abilities as a team is key to your success. The resulting series of feints, advances, retreats and more is great fun. The free-to-play Pokémon Unite follows that template, but simplifies the formula making it much easier to learn.

Two teams of five do battle, with each player controlling one of 20 playable Pokémon, which in turn are split into five battle classes. As they level-up, they go through familiar evolutions, too. Battles last 10 minutes, with players earning Aeos Energy by defeating AI units and completing goals (like finding wild Pokémon) to decide the winner. It's a shame you can boost some stats via microtransactions, but overall, this is a robust, accessible and addictive entry into the genre.

Puyo Puyo Tetris 2

Age Range = All | **Local Multiplayer** = Yes
Difficulty = Easy | **Genre** = Puzzle

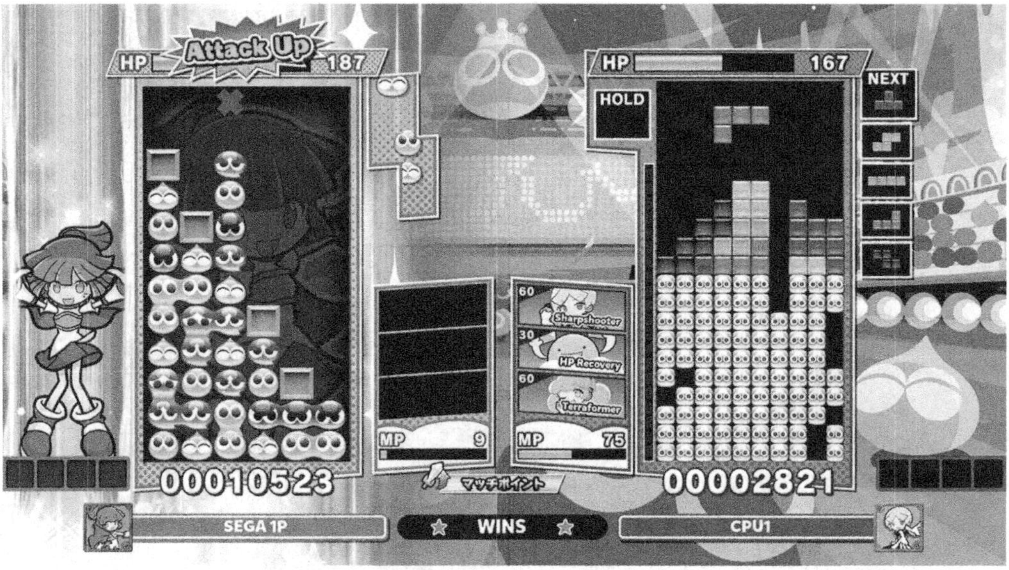

The game of Tetris needs little introduction; different shaped blocks fall from the top of the stage and you need to puzzle them together as neatly as possible. It's legendary. You may not be familiar with Puyo, however. It's a similar style of puzzle game, except the goal is to match up rows or columns of different coloured Puyo so they disappear.

This game combines these experiences together and then gives them a cutesy, text-heavy story as well. The new additions in this sequel add nicely to the base gameplay established in the 2014 original.

There are now Skill Battles, whereby items and skills based on the character impact the gameplay. There's an Adventure Mode, too, which involves an overworld you can roam with characters to challenge in Skill Battles. There's been a notable improvement to multiplayer, too, with greater depth in modes and easier league play.

Both games were already a lot of fun and adding them together gives each a boost. It's just a shame about the cheesy music!

Skater XL

Age Range = All | **Local Multiplayer** = No
Difficulty = Hard | **Genre** = Sports

The coolest thing about skateboarding is that flow you get when you're in the zone. Where the deck feel glued to your feet and you can cruise down the street, weaving in and out of obstacles, leaping gaps, grinding walls and pulling off tricks.

In the old days, video games tried to capture that with just button presses, but it didn't feel right. Then the Skate series came along and added physics-based tricks, using the sticks. Skater XL takes it another step further, with no set tricks or grinds built into the game. Instead, your skater reacts to the way you move and where you go in a more realistic, freeform way.

It takes quite a while to get used to, but if you stick with it, the gameplay becomes a lot of fun and makes you feel like a pro skater. It's a bit of a shame the game launched with only one location in Los Angeles, but the world is detailed and features real spots to hit. Plus, it's cool you can play as some pro skaters, or customise your own pro and board.

SMURFS: MISSION VILEAF, THE

Age Range = All | **Local Multiplayer** = Yes
Difficulty = Easy | **Genre** = 3D Platformer

The Smurfs have got their own 3D adventure game. There are few cuter stars on TV and in cinemas than the little blue tree huggers and it should only take you one quick look at the screenshots to know that their world has been wonderfully recreated in this game. Just exploring the village and the forest, as well as the game's five worlds, is fun enough for fans of the series.

But there's a cool story as wel.

Naturally, the latest pitfalls to fall on the Smurfs are the result of evil wizard Gargamel. This time he has created a toxic plant — the Vileaf — that he has let loose on the forest. Not only is it corrupting and poisoning other plants, but its seeds lure in Smurfs and then entrap them. How horrible, right?

Papa Smurf is on the case, however. He knows of an antidote, but it requires special ingredients in order to be made. So, it's up to you to go and find these ingredients, while rescuing trapped Smurfs and poisoned plants on the way.

The four heroes that go on this mission are Smurfette, Hefty, Brainy and Chef. So, there's a good mix of characters to enjoy and master. And the great news is that you can play in co-op, which is always our favourite way to play.

The moment-to-moment action is just what you might expect from a 3D platformer. Think Super Mario, Crash Bandicoot, Ratchet & Clank and Skylanders. That kind of experience.

So, you're not just exploring, collecting and defeating enemies, but also trying to puzzle your way around obstacles.

Most of the controls and combat tie into a unique and cool tool called the Smurfizer. This is your main tool for saving

the day in The Smurfs: Mission Leaf has been created by none other than Handy Smurf.

The Smurfizer looks like a mix between a vacuum, a gramophone and the Ghostbusters Proton pack. This awesome tool can do a stack of different things and how you not just master its abilities, but find items to upgrade its skills, is key to success.

First and foremost, The Smurfizer can be used to heal plants by spraying antidote on bushes and flowers that have been poisoned by Gargamel's Vileaf. But you can also use it as a movement tool. It can help you dash forward at speed.

You can also use it to glide over long distances. Plus, it's important in combat. You can use it to dive bomb on threats or obstacles, or use it to suck in objects to then shoot at foes.

It's impossible not to love The Smurfs. If there are a fan of the cartoons or movies in your home, they'll no doubt really enjoy this game. Especially if they have a friend of sibling to play it with.

Sonic Colors Ultimate

Age Range = All | **Local Multiplayer** = Yes
Difficulty = Medium | **Genre** = Adventure platformer

It's hard to believe given the recent success of the Sonic the Hedgehog films, but during the 2000s, the blue speedster really lost his way.

For a moment there, it even looked like the legendary game hero would fade away into obscurity. Then Sonic Colors arrived in 2010 on the Nintendo Wii and brought the series back to life.

Developer Team Sonic finally got the 3D gameplay right, with a mix of fantastic, flashy levels and a story telling the

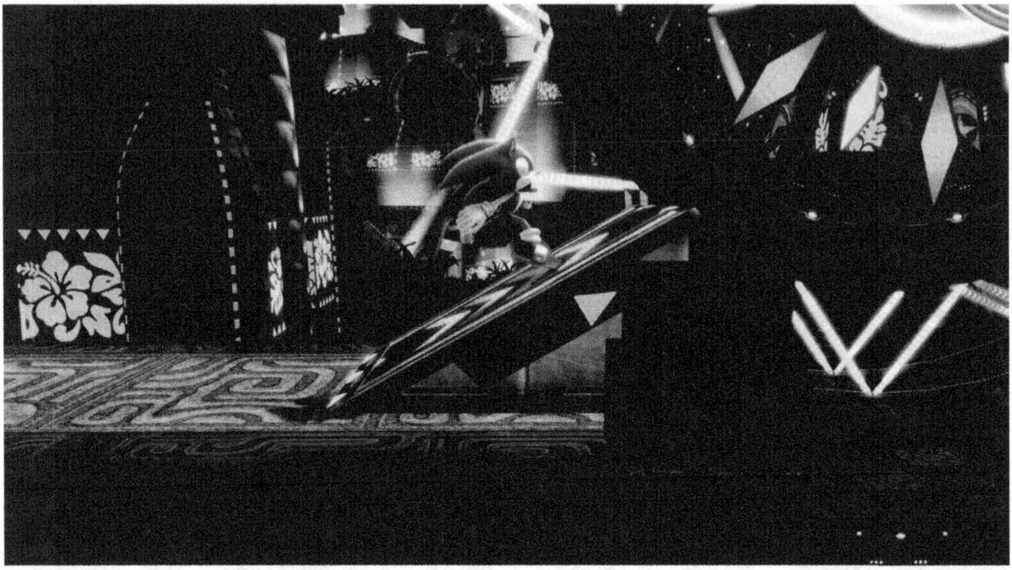

origin of a new set of characters, the Wisps. If you've played any of the subsequent games in the series, the Wisps will be familiar. These coloured critters grant Sonic new abilities, mixing up the traditional Sonic gameplay in all the right ways.

For its reimagining on Nintendo Switch, the visuals, controls and audio have all been greatly improved. There are now customisation options and a rescue feature where Tails can pull you up if you fall off a ledge (as long as you've found a Tails token).

Plus, the Jade Ghost wisp, introduced in 2019's Team Sonic Racing, has been added to the game with its ability to let you pass through objects. A Rival Rush mode also adds head-to-head multiplayer! Great additions to an already solid game.

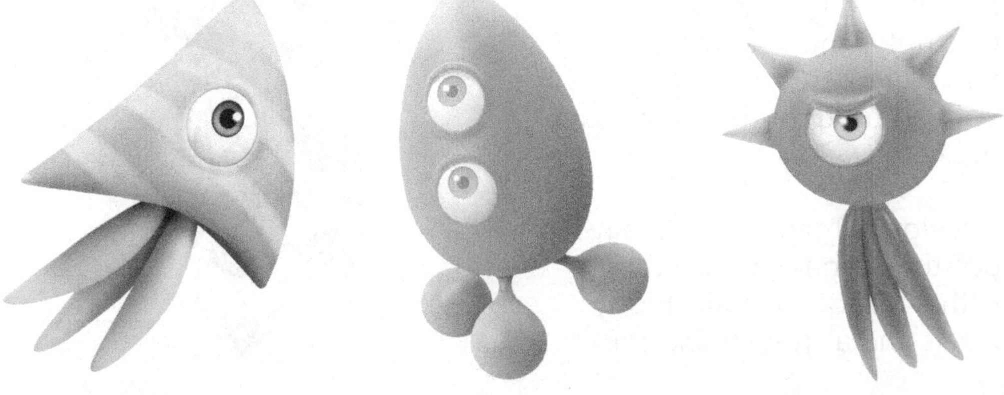

SpongeBob SquarePants: Battle for Bikini Bottom Rehydrated

Age Range = All | **Local Multiplayer** = Yes
Difficulty = Easy | **Genre** = Adventure

There's no shortage of remakes hitting all consoles at the moment, but we've been pretty happy with the games that have been selected for a new lease on life. Like this classic 3D platforming adventure from back in 2003, right in the middle of the genre's heyday.

All the action takes place at the bottom of the ocean and exploring this extremely colourful and detailed world is a lot of fun. A large part of that, of course, is thanks to the characters.

You can play as SpongeBob, Patrick and Sandy, revolving between their special abilities as required and laughing at their silliness. Of which there's plenty as you complete your goal of destroying an army of robots and their boss, Thwart Plankton.

The original game was already great, but I am really happy with the improvements to the controls and the visuals. It's also nice that a new Horde mode has been added so there is multiplayer, online or splitscreen, to enjoy, too. Welcome back, SpongeBob.

SUBNAUTICA: BELOW ZERO

Age Range = Middle | **Local Multiplayer** = No
Difficulty = Medium | **Genre** = Survival Adventure

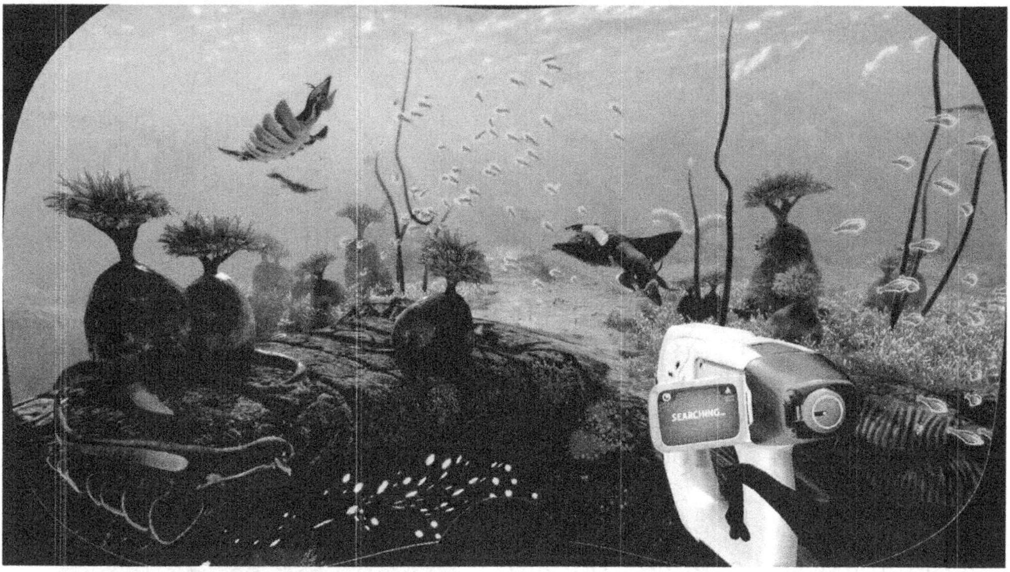

The first Subnautica game was one of my favourite releases of this generation. It's a survival game like no other. It started with you crash landing on a planet covered in water. You had to swim around, learning about all the strange creatures and the landscape. You then needed to harvest resources and use these to craft better technology, so you could explore deeper into the ocean.

All this while unravelling the mystery of what happened to cause such widespread flooding on the planet.

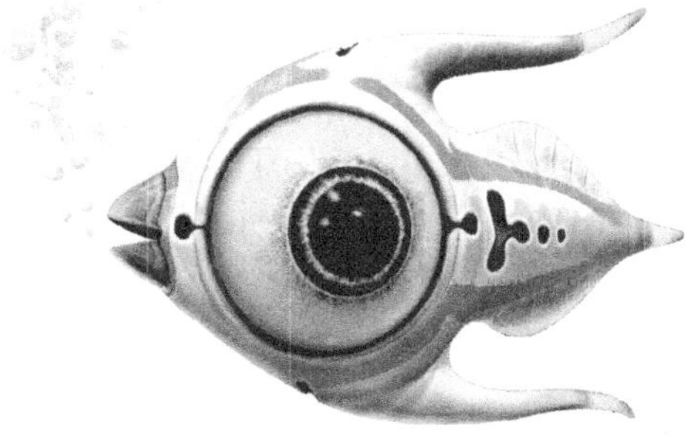

This sequel takes everything up a notch. It's set on a new planet which, as the title suggests, is much colder. Its oceans are also a lot deeper and filled with all new creatures and flora to discover.

The game is still played from the first-person view, but there have been lots of great improvements. There's now a day-night cycle and dynamic weather. There are more alien structures to discover and explore. There's now a large part of the open world that is on land that you walk around on. You can craft bigger structures, too.

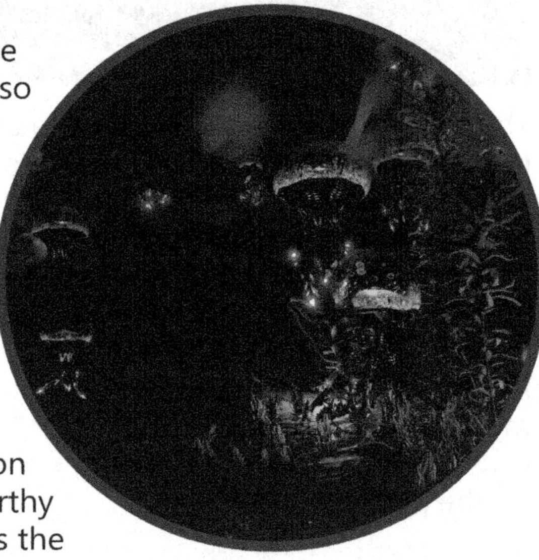

Plus, you don't just need to survive hunger, thirst and enemies, but also the temperature. It's an awesome run of new additions.

It's worth noting that the first game in the Subnautica series released on Switch at the same time as this sequel.

It didn't get a Switch release at the time that it originally arrived on other consoles, and it's totally worthy checking out as well. The sequel is the better game, but only just.

Super Mario 3D All-Stars

Age Range = All | **Local Multiplayer** = Yes
Difficulty = Easy | **Genre** = Arcade

Way back in the SNES era, the coolest game you could get was Super Mario All-Stars. It came with three games from the series bundled together, providing hours of awesome gaming. Decades later and Nintendo is doing it again, this time bundling three other iconic games from yesteryear and putting it on the Switch.

The oldest is legendary 1996 N64 game Super Mario 64. Then there is 2002 GameCube open-world classic Super Mario Sunshine. Followed by the brilliant Wii game Super Mario Galaxy from 2007. The latter is the only one with co-op multiplayer, with the first two games being single player only.

Of course, the graphics have been sharpened, the great soundtracks

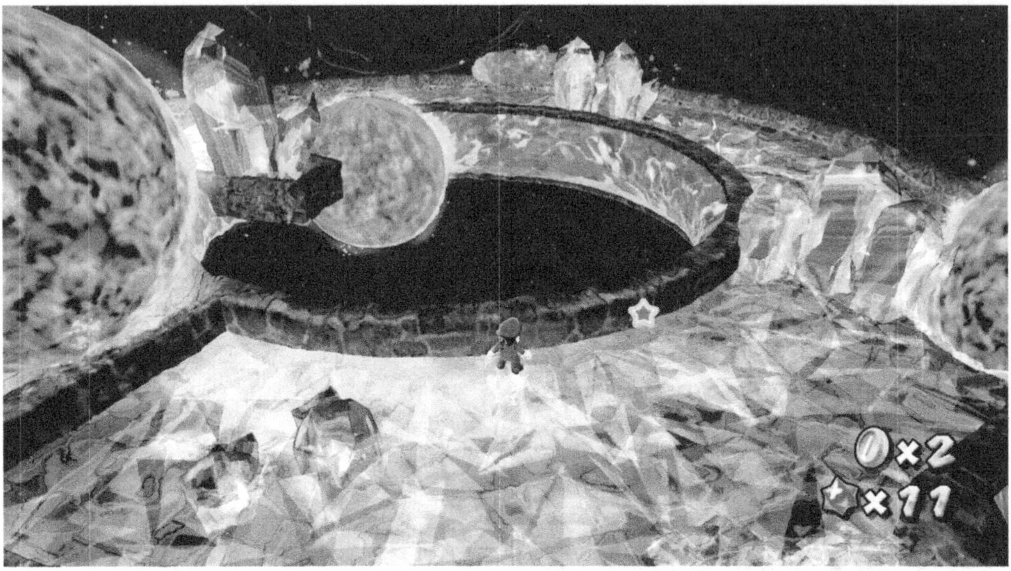

remastered, and the gameplay improved for the Switch. They don't look modern, but they're still a lot crisper to look at and faster to play than they once were. It would have been nice if they were fully remade, but this is still a chance to play three brilliant Mario games for the one price. How could you not love that?!

But it's not all good news. Surprisingly, Nintendo only made this game available for a limited time. You can still find some physical copies out in the wild, but the game can't currently be bought digitally. It seems like such a waste, however, we're sure that Nintendo will make Super Mario 3D All-Stars available again sometime in the future.

Super Mario 3D World + Bowser's Fury

Age Range = All | **Local Multiplayer** = Yes
Difficulty = Medium | **Genre** = Platformer

It's been quite a treat seeing so many classic Wii U getting a new lease on life on Switch. Here comes another one, and it's a fantastic entry in the Super Mario platformer series. Super Mario 3D World has some truly brilliant levels rich with imagination and detail as you might expect from the maestros at Nintendo. But this time, the gameplay focuses on co-op.

You and three friends (offline or online) move through the isometric world, facing off against many enemies while finding secret areas and power-ups. The latter includes the amazing cat suit!

It's a fantastic game, but there's more. For this remake there is a whole additional expansion to enjoy called Bowser's Fury. It provides more levels with a much darker theme, adding in cool new features like weather effects. This makes a great game even better value for money.

Tony Hawk's Pro Skater 1 + 2

Age Range = Middle | **Local Multiplayer** = Yes
Difficulty = Medium | **Genre** = Extreme Sports

A remake of the first two Tony Hawk games has landed. Sometimes remakes feel their age, but that's not the case with this game. Both included titles have been entirely remade in a new game engine, so both the visuals and the killer soundtrack feel modern.

All 19 levels from the classic games return, too, so there's been no shortcuts taken. In a nice touch, new moves have been included that we didn't see in the original titles, as well as the Create-A-Skater and Create-a-Park modes. So yes, you can build your own skate park!

There's even splitscreen and online multiplayer. If that wasn't enough, the original 13 skaters are back in the game, however, they look like they do now. As in, seriously old dudes!

TRANSFORMERS: BATTLEGROUNDS

Age Range = Middle | **Local Multiplayer** = Yes
Difficulty = Medium | **Genre** = Survival Adventure

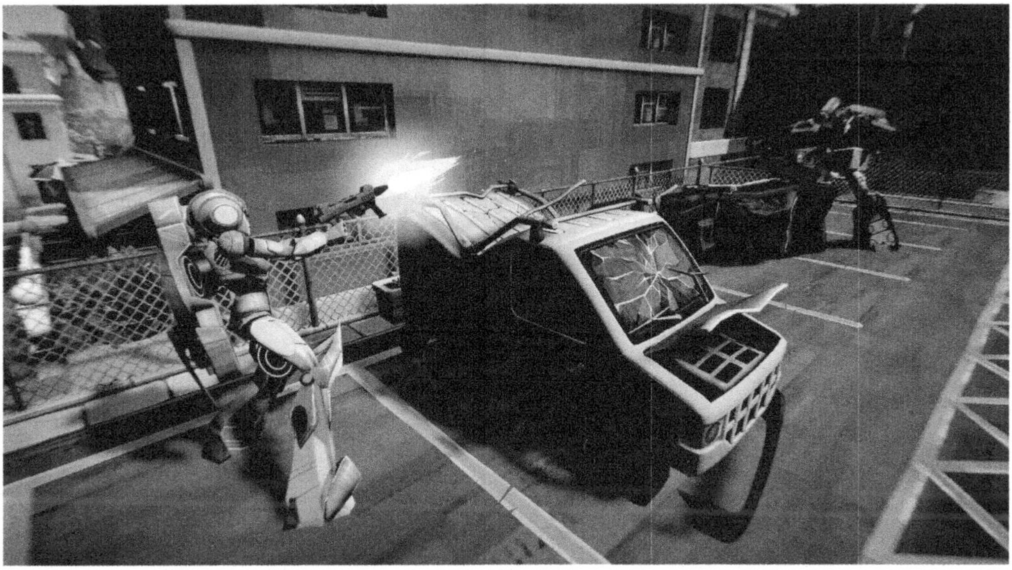

It's always awesome to play as Bumblebee, Optimus Prime, Grimlock, Arcee, Windblade and co. But this is a different experience to the usual third-person action-adventure Transformers games I've played.

Battlegrounds is a strategy game focused on tactical warfare. You assemble a squad of Autobots before each stage and then head into turn-based combat where you spend action points to move, defend or attack, as well as build up to special abilities. Positioning your soldiers to avoid destructible objects in the environment or use combo attacks is key to beating Megatron's Decepticons baddies.

The visuals aren't spectacular, but it's kind of cool looking down on a cartoon city from above and seeing all the different battles playing out. And while it doesn't look like much is going on, there is surprising depth to the strategy. A fact that becomes even more clear in co-op!

WarioWare: Get It Together

Age Range = All | **Local Multiplayer** = Yes
Difficulty = Easy | **Genre** = Party

The dastardly Wario has been twirling his villainous moustache in Mario's direction since the Game Boy era, but he's become better known this century for his WarioWare titles.

This series takes the idea of a minigame quite literally, providing a catalogue of fast-paced, chaotic and frequently whacky experiences to compete in that are over in a matter of seconds.

In each level the long wick on a bomb is burning towards its explosive conclusion and you need to complete the minigame before it goes boom!

This, the tenth entry in the series, sticks true to that formula. And it's as silly as ever. One moment you will be dodging bird poo dropping down from overhanging wires.

The next you will be flying on a jetpack trying to nudge two aliens hanging off vines towards each other so they can kiss! Or you may be mining boogers out of giant nose. You get the idea, right?

There is a story mode, but really this is about laughing and playing with friends. There's 12 characters to choose from and in a first for the series, they behave differently. So, you can form a squad and be thrust randomly into the shoes of different characters as you play the same minigames, changing up the experience.

Plus there's now some co-op minigames where two players need to work together to beat the bomb.

The very Japanese visuals and 2D worlds are kid friendly as that's the audience Nintendo is aiming for. So while there's a lot of variety in WarioWare: Get It Together, it's not the deepest experience and better suited to younger gamers.

WHAT THE GOLF?

Age Range = All | **Local Multiplayer** = Yes
Difficulty = Easy | **Genre** = Sport

This game is almost impossible to describe. Well except for the golf part — you understand how golf works, I'm assuming? Well, this game takes the core concept of the sport, rolls it with its tongue into the corner of its cheek and then chews on it for a bit.

The idea is to still hit something down the fairway and into the hole — or against the flag in this case — at the end of the course. You do this by aiming in the right direction and then controlling a power bar to judge the distance. However, every level the weirdest possible obstacles or objects to hit are added to the game, keeping you not only playing, but laughing for hours.

For example, in one level you're not aiming a ball, but a cow that is on a swing. You pull the swing back and then push it forward to shoot the cow at the distant flag. In another you are shooting a remote-controlled car.

As you get deeper into the game, more mechanics are added, and the objects change keeping you constantly guessing at what is coming next. And everything has this ragdoll physics effect, too — think Goat Simulator or Humans Fall Flat! So, it really is funny doing just about anything. What the golf indeed!

WILDFIRE

Age Range = Older | **Local Multiplayer** = No
Difficulty = Medium | **Genre** = Platformer

There were two reasons why I was excited for this game. First of all, it's made by a small indie developer team in Sydney, Australia — my hometown. Second, it focuses on stealth platforming gameplay where one of your main weapons is lighting fires.

Lighting fires is fun, especially when it has believable impacts on the game world and its occupants. Why? Because it allows you to think up cool and fun strategies for making your way past enemies without being seen. And fire propagation is just the start. There are other elements you can control, too. Like water and earth. And you can combine them! For example, you can trap an enemy in vines and then set the vines on fire. Nasty!

Your abilities get upgraded as you play and it's really cool how the developer has got the NPCs to respond to your actions in believable ways. There's just so much depth to this medieval world. You can play the game in co-op for added awesome, and the retro visual style is detailed and beautiful. An indie gem.

WINDBOUND

Age Range = Middle | **Local Multiplayer** = No
Difficulty = Medium | Genre = Survival

This is a survival game, but it has a similar feel to open-world adventure title The Legend of Zelda: Breath of the Wild. That alone should have you excited! You find yourself in the shoes of Kara, left to survive alone on an island. As you explore you will fight off beasts, find resources to craft better equipment, hunt for food and upgrade your abilities.

Your main transportation is a boat and as you improve it, the further you can sail. This is where the real sense of adventure should begin as you take to the sea. Although its hampered somewhat by the hands-on nature of the sailing and the slow upgrade path. These can make it a bit tedious at first.

Sadly, the game is also let down by the lack of truly interesting things to discover as you come across new islands. They're randomly generated, so lack that sense of purpose and character we saw in a game like The Legend of Zelda: Wind Waker where every island is handcrafted. But at least it's unpredictable, meaning the decisions you make on which island to go to next can really impact your survival.

Despite my gripes, Windbound remains good fun for the kids. And I like how you're always working towards solving the mystery of what happened to the ancient people who used to live on this archipelago. That keeps you going.

Wonder Boy: Asha in Monster World

Age Range = All | **Local Multiplayer** = No
Difficulty = Easy | **Genre** = Platformer

Back in 1994, a fourth game in the brilliant Wonder Boy sidescrolling platformer series came out, but not in Western markets. Which was such a shame.

The three previous games were classics and the fourth game mixed things up by making the lead character a girl. Which considering the era it was made, was a brave and pioneering move.

Her name is Asha, she is armed with a sword and she's great at taking down monsters. Her goal is to save some spirits who have been calling out for help, and she does get some aid from a genie.

This series was one of the first platformers to mix genres, adding in RPG and action-adventure elements to the gameplay.

You need to talk to other citizens, upgrade your equipment and even summon a pet to help you traverse the land and survive falling rocks.

The good news,as you may have guessed, is that gamers outside Japan finally have a chance to experience Wonder Boy IV. This newly released remaster rebuilds the game from the ground-up, giving it brand new graphics and music, and adding voices to the cutscenes. It's simple gaming by today's standards, but still fun.

Worms Rumble

Age Range = Middle | **Local Multiplayer** = No
Difficulty = Medium | **Genre** = Battle Royale

The Worms games are so awesome. In the past, they've been focused on four teams of four worms randomly spawning in a randomly generated map. Their goal is to be the last worm standing and you have an arsenal of crazy weapons to help you get your way. Watching worms and chunks of the world get blown away by banana bombs, concrete donkeys, exploding sheep and the like is hilarious.

This new game keeps the same sense of humour, fun and weaponised mayhem, but completely changes the idea of last worm standing. Now it's more of a Battle Royale scenario.

Instead of each player taking turns to attack with their worm, there are now 30 players going crazy in real-time. As a result, the worms move much faster and the levels no longer disintegrate. It's a bit like a Super Smash Bros with worms!

So, while putting the focus of combat on reflexes and quick thinking makes it less about strategy and more about action, it's still lots of fun.

WWE 2K Battlegrounds

Age Range = Middle | **Local Multiplayer** = Yes
Difficulty = Medium | **Genre** = Sports

In 2020, 2K Games skipped its usual wrestling sim and opted for a spin-off in WWE 2K Battlegrounds. It ended up being a masterstroke. It took away the seriousness — if you can imagine anything being serious about WWE — resulting in an experience that's a lot more fun.

Rather than taking a straight-faced, simulation-like approach to wrestling, WWE 2K Battleground instead goes fully over-the-top. From the visual style right down to the moves, it's all focused on being fast and funny at the same time.

There's still plenty of familiar faces, including recent stars and legends from yesteryear, to control in four-player battles. But moves are made much easier to access and unleash and it's great just how silly they've gone with the abilities.

For example, you can throw opponents well into the air, smash them with motorbikes and even feed them to crocodiles. It makes for one of the best games to play with your friends on Switch.

Nintendo On Mobile

Recently, Nintendo has been doing a lot more to spread its wings beyond its own consoles. In particular, we've started to see a number of Nintendo brands appearing on mobiles. Who could forget the mega global blockbuster Pokémon Go, for example? Super Mario Run and Animal Crossing: Pocket Camp were also early mobile success stories. So, what else from the Nintendo universe can you find on mobiles? Here's a few to check out.

Mario Kart Tour (iOS, Android)

It's true! The most legendary of all karting series has arrived on mobile phones. Mario and all his pals from the Mushroom Kingdom bring the classic tracks, power-ups and power-sliding fun to mobile devices with some new tricks.

As well as classic tracks, for example, there are also new circuits based on real-world locations. These change every two weeks, too, giving you a great reason to keep coming back to the game.

Elsewhere there is a new Frenzy Mode that makes you invincible and gives you an unlimited supply of a power-ups for a short amount of time. You'll also find bonus challenges to complete, like one where you face off against Mega Bowser. Plus, the racing is simple to control; you can even play with just one hand!

Mario Kart Tour is free to download and start playing, but there are microtransactions, which includes a host of customisation options for characters and karts. So, be careful what you buy.

Pokémon Masters (iOS, Android)

The developer of Pokémon has flipped the legendary series on its head with this new mobile game. Instead of collecting colourful critters, you're collecting famous trainers from all throughout the series' history.

When you find a trainer and recruit them to your team, they come with their own Pokémon. You level-up the trainer of course, and while you can't change their Pokémon, you can mega evolve them. This improves their stats for combat and fighting is like most other Pokémon games, if slightly more basic. There's more fun to be had in seeing the characters interact in the gorgeous story elements and scouting out new Trainers.

Thankfully, while you can buy random character/Pokémon drops with microtransactions, you gain access to plenty of content for free. You can finish the whole game without spending a cent! And once you beat the story, rather than just grinding away levelling-up, there is a co-op mode you can jump into. Well worth a look!

Pokémon Rumble Rush (iOS, Android)

It was quite a surprise when this the new Pokémon game turned up on mobile, not Switch. But it's not an RPG, either. It's a brawler where you jump into an island environment and battle your way through swarms

of enemies capturing Pokémon. Play well and you'll get to face off against the Super Bosses.

Every two weeks the island changes, which means you can come back and catch different types of Pokémon in new environments. You can switch between Pokémon mid-battle, so the strategy is to make sure you are always using the best critter type.

You can let your Pokémon fight automatically, but you get better results if you take control of the attacks and dodges.

You can upgrade and level-up your Pokémon, too, plus there is multiplayer and a few other different modes to explore. It can get a bit repetitive, and there are in-app purchases to avoid, but this game is still solid fun.

Dr. Mario World (iOS, Android)

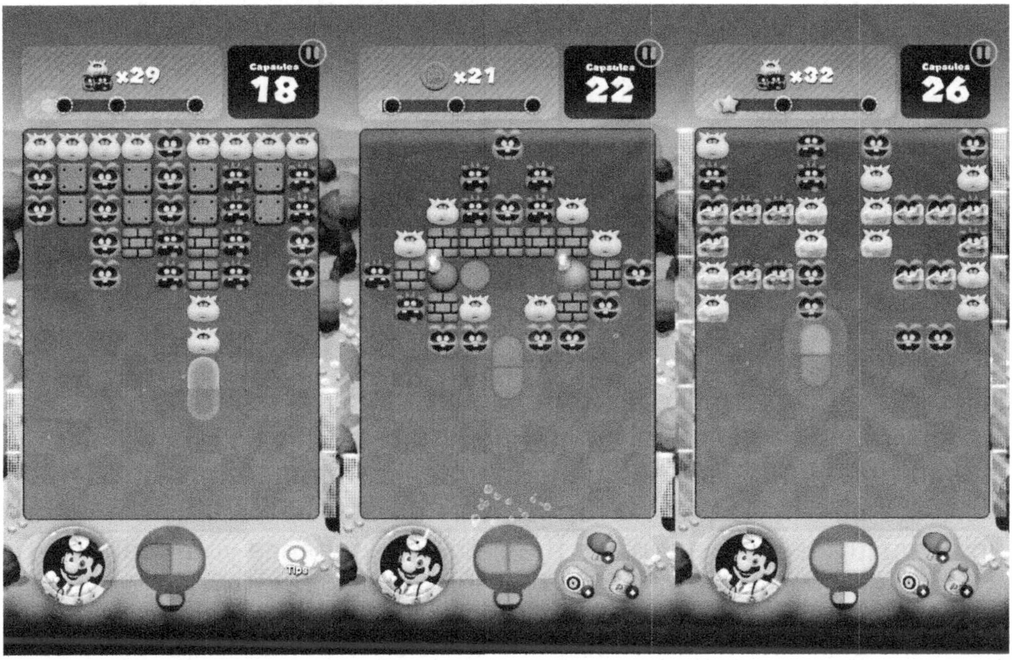

Back in 1990, Nintendo came out with the awesome Dr. Mario game in response to the success of Tetris. It was a match-three game where you needed to guide coloured pills down through a space so they would land on, and destroy, viruses.

Nintendo has now re-imagined this idea for mobiles and come up with gameplay that feels familiar, but also suits a touchscreen. Now you swipe capsules onto the screen and instead of them falling down, they go up. You can then drag the capsule around, or tap to spin it, so that it lands in the best spot.

Also, you only have a limited number of capsules per stage, and obstacles to negotiate, which keep things challenging. With 200 stages, various other characters to play (like Dr. Bowser and Dr. Toad) and some smart multiplayer features, this is a great mobile game.

Pikmin Bloom (IOS, Android)

Niantic, the developers of Pokémon Go, released a new game in late 2021 that once again involved a Nintendo title. This time it was the Pikmin, and yes, it's still an augmented reality game. Although the word "game" may be going too far. This is less of a game and more of an interactive exercise app. It's the type of experience you might play when you are walking to a friend's house or to school.

As you'd expect, the game stars the plant-based Pikmin creatures, which in the main games follow you around and can be ordered about to complete tasks based on their special abilities.

This game features the same cheery music and visuals of the main titles. You start with one red Pikmin. It follows you as you walk through the real world, finding more Pikmin, fruit and flower petals. You can feed the nectar from the fruit to your Pikmin to grow the flower on its head. But more interesting are the flower petals.

You can use these to plant flowers as you walk, leaving trails in the real world you can follow, and other players can also see. Then if you come across a giant flower bud, you and other players must put petals around it to help it bloom. The number of steps you make in any day also helps you level-up, encouraging you to exercise more. So, while there's isn't a lot of game here, it still makes the tedium of walking much more exciting.

How to play retro games on Nintendo Switch

In late 2021, Nintendo expanded its Nintendo Switch Online offering. If you pay more, you get more. It's not a great approach in my opinion; the company should be rewarding its members, not gouging them for more money on games that long since made a whopping profit. But anyway, that's Nintendo for you.

You're free to get the existing Nintendo Switch Online subscription, the price of which hasn't changed. But if you pay double the price, you can get the Nintendo Switch Online + Expansion pack. To be fair, it's still quite cheap even with the expansion pass. Cheaper than both the Xbox and PlayStation online passes, anyway. I won't quote you a price though, as it varies per country.

With so many exciting new games coming to the Switch, I struggle to encourage my kids to be interested in games that look and play like they were made decades ago. Short of educating them on gaming's legacy, or getting a bunch of games for a relatively small price, you could give the Expansion Pass a miss. Unless, of course, it's for your own nostalgia.

N64

For your extra money, you get access to these N64 games as of mid-2023, with more to be added later. All good games: in fact, some of the best of all time.

- Banjo-Kazooie
- Dr. Mario 64
- F-Zero X
- GolenEye 007
- Kirby 64: The Crystal Shards
- Legend of Zelda: Majora's Mask, The
- Legend of Zelda: Ocarina of Time, The
- Mario Golf
- Mario Kart 64
- Mario Party
- Mario Party 2
- Mario Tennis
- Paper Mario
- Pilotwings 64
- Pokémon Puzzle League

- Pokémon Snap
- Pokémon Stadium
- Sin & Punishment
- Star Fox 64
- Super Mario 64
- Wave Race 64
- WinBack: Covert Operations
- Yoshi's Story

As of the time of writing, the following N64 games were announced, but not yet available. Mario Party 3, Pokémon Stadium 2, 1080° Snowboarding and Excitebike 64.

Sega Mega Drive

It's not just the N64. You also get the following Sega Mega Drive games. Those with long memories will know it as the other great video game console of the early 1990s.

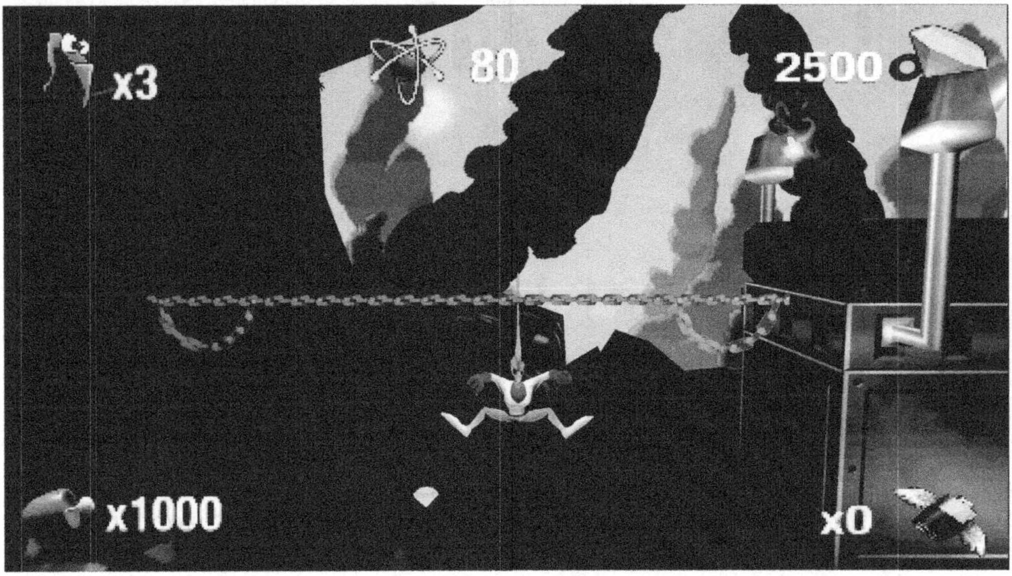

- Alien Soldier
- Alisa Dragoon
- Altered Beast
- Beyond Oasis
- Castlevania Bloodlines
- Comix Zone
- Contra Hard Corps
- Dr Robotnik's Mean Bean Machine
- Dynamite Headdy
- Earthworm Jim
- Ecco The Dolphin
- Flicky
- Golden Axe
- Gunstar Heroes
- Kid Chameleon
- Light Crusader
- Mega Man: The Wily Wars
- Musha

- Phantasy Star IV
- Pulseman
- Ristar
- Shining Force
- Shinobi III: Return of the Ninja Master
- Sonic The Hedgehog 2
- Street Fighter II: Super Champion Edition
- Streets of Rage 2
- Strider
- Super Fantasy Zone
- Sword of Vermilion
- Target Earth
- Thunder Force II
- ToeJam & Earl
- Zero Wing

- Wave Race 64
- WinBack: Covert Operations
- Yoshi's Story

Game Boy and Game Boy Advance

There's a handful of games from the beloved Game Boy handheld included, too.

- Alone in the Dark: The New Nightmare (GB)
- Blaster Master: Enemy Below (GB)
- Fire Emblem: The Blinding Blade (GBA)
- Game & Watch Gallery 3 (GB)
- Gargoyle's Quest (GB)
- Kirby's Dream Land (GB)
- Kirby Tilt 'n' Tumble (GB)
- Kuru Kuru Kururin (GBA)

- Legend of Zelda: Link's Awakening DX, The (GB)
- Legend of Zelda: The Minish Cap, The (GBA)
- Mario & Luigi: Superstar Saga (GBA)
- Mario Kart: Super Circuit (GBA)
- Metroid II - Return of Samus (GB)
- Super Mario Advance 4: Super Mario Bros. 3 (GBA)
- Super Mario Land 2: 6 Golden Coins (GB)
- Tetris (GB)
- Wario Land 3 (GB)
- WarioWare, Inc.: Minigame Mania (GBA)

Flagged for arrival from Game Boy Advance at some point, possibly by the time you read this, are; Kirby & The Amazing Mirror, Golden Sun, F-Zero Maximum Velocity. And from the original Game Boy, Pokémon Trading Card Game, The Legend of Zelda: Oracle of Ages and The Legend of Zelda: Oracle of Seasons.

SNES

The Super Nintendo Entertainment System is a personal favourite of mine. It wasn't my first console — that honour goes to the Commodore 64 — but it was the first I bought with my own money as an eager 12-year-old.

There are a stack of games from the system you can play on Switch. And it includes some of the system's best.

- Bombuzal
- Brawl Brothers
- Breath Of Fire
- Breath of Fire II
- Claymates
- Congo's Caper
- Demon's Crest
- Doomsday Warrior
- Donkey Kong Country
- Donkey Kong Country 2: Diddy's Kong-Quest
- Donkey Kong Country 3: Dixie Kong's Double Trouble!
- EarthBound
- Earthworm Jim 2
- F-Zero

- Fighter's History
- Harvest Moon
- Ignition Factor, The
- JellyBoy
- Joe & Mac (aka Caveman Ninja)
- Joe & Mac 2: Lost in the Tropics
- Kirby's Avalanche
- Kirby's Dream Course
- Kirby's Dream Land 3
- Kirby Super Star
- Legend of Zelda: A Link to the Past, The
- Magical Drop 2
- Mario's Super Picross
- Natsume Championship Wrestling
- Operation Logic Bomb
- Panel de Pon
- Peace Keepers, The
- Pilotwings
- Pop'n TwinBee
- Prehistorik Man
- Psycho Dream
- Rival Turf!
- Spanky's Quest
- Star Fox
- Star Fox 2
- Stunt Race FX
- Super Baseball Simulator 1.000
- Super E.D.F: Earth Defense Force
- Super Ghouls'n Ghosts
- Super Mario All-Stars
- Super Mario Kart
- Super Mario World
- Super Mario World 2: Yoshi's Island
- Super Metroid
- Super Punch-Out!!
- Super Puyo Puyo 2
- Super Soccer
- Super Tennis
- Smash Tennis
- Super Valis IV
- Tuff E Nuff
- Wild Guns

NES

You can heard back to where it all began for many of the greatest game series in history with the NES catalogue. In many cases, you can play through the whole history of Nintendo's most beloved characters across the retro games the Switch has on offer. Although it may only be your parents, or even grandparents, who remember these titles.

- Adventures of Lolo
- Balloon Fight
- Baseball
- Blaster Master
- City Connection
- Clu Clu Land
- Crystalis
- Daiva Story 6: Imperial of Nirsartia
- Dig Dug II
- Donkey Kong
- Donkey Kong 3
- Donkey Kong Jr.
- Double Dragon
- Double Dragon II: The Revenge
- Dr. Mario
- EarthBound Beginnings

- Eliminator Boat Duel
- Excitebike
- Fire 'n Ice
- Ghosts'n Goblins
- Gradius
- Ice Climber
- Ice Hockey
- JOURNEY TO SILIUS
- Kid Icarus
- Kirby's Adventure
- Kung-Fu Heroes
- Mappy-Land
- Mario Bros.
- Metroid
- Mighty Bomb Jack
- Mystery Tower
- NES Open Tournament Golf
- Nightshade
- Ninja Gaiden
- Ninja JaJaMaru-kun
- Pinball
- Pro Wrestling
- Punch-Out!! Featuring Mr. Dream
- River City Ransom
- Rygar
- S.C.A.T.: Special Cybernetic Attack Team
- Shadow of the Ninja
- Soccer
- Solomon's Key
- Star Soldier
- StarTropics
- Super Dodge Ball
- Super Mario Bros.
- Super Mario Bros. 2
- Super Mario Bros. 3
- Super Mario Bros: The Lost Levels
- Tecmo Bowl
- Tennis
- Immortal, The
- Legend of Zelda, The
- TwinBee
- Vice: Project Doom
- Volleyball
- VS. Excitebike
- Wario's Woods
- Wrecking Crew
- Yoshi
- Zelda II: The Adventure of Link

OTHER BONUSES

When you get the Nintendo Switch Online + Expansion Pass pack, it's not just retro games you gain access to. For starters, you also get the Happy Home Paradise DLC pack for Animal Crossing: New Horizon. It's a great game, but if you don't have it, the DLC isn't much use to you.

If you own Mario Kart Deluxe 8, you'll get the Booster Course Pass, which adds a whopping 48 new circuits to the game. They're all remastered classics from previous titles.

The Splatoon 2 Octo Expansion is yet another bonus. Again, you need to be playing the game to get any benefit, and it has been superseded by Splatoon 3. The DLC gives you 80 underground test facilities to navigate, and the ability to play as an Octoling in multiplayer games.

More to Come

If you're wondering why some of the recent big releases on Switch aren't in this book, it's because I'm hard at work on Volume 3. It will be out very soon, and will join my books on PlayStation 5 and upcoming titles focused on Xbox Series X and Meta Quest.

To make sure you're on top of every Old Mate Media release, sign-up to the newsletter by emailing books@oldmatemedia.com now.

We also have plenty of other great books to explore. Make sure you check out our sci-fi series **Adam X**, which is very much inspired by a mix of video games like Mass Effect and movies like Star Wars.

If you're a parent, we also have a stack of great picture books, cookbooks and activities guides, too. Plus, we can help you turn your book into a reality should you dream of being a published author.

Made in United States
North Haven, CT
21 October 2024

59263035R00089